LETTERS TO PEARL

BOOK 1

THE COURTSHIP

Book One

Copyright © 2014 Pearl Rose
All rights reserved.
ISBN-10:1500667641
ISBN-13:978-1500667641

DEDICATION

The Lord has directed the transcribing and writing of this book so seekers who want to know Him with greater intimacy can discover what that looks like in the life of a believer and how to press in for more of Him.

It is only for those who want more than church, more than religion, more than "typical Christianity." It is for those who want intimacy with the Father, His Son Jesus, and Holy Spirit.

If you are satisfied with what you already have, then that is fine. This book is only for those who want more. It is for those who want to be, not typical Christians, but followers of Jesus.

Book One

TABLE OF CONTENTS

Personal Letter from the Original Pearl 1
The Purpose of the Pearl Letters 3

PROLOGUE
Love - the Fullness of God 9
Spots and Wrinkles 13
Come to Me - No Boundaries 19
Purified 22
Washed 24
Bear One Another's Burden 27
Parable of the Ten Lepers 30
By the Will of God 35
Let Me Build Your House 39
I Am Your New Reality 41
You Died for Me Today 44
His Presence 46

CHAPTERS
Abandon All for Me 51
Holy Spirit Speaks 52
Restoring His Image 53
His Peace 55
His Pleasure 56
Choice Words Are Few 58
True Sacrifice Involves Pain 59
Overwhelmed by Him 64
Lovesick for Jesus 68
The Circle of Love 70
Chip Away 72
Let Go of Everything 74
Papa Speaks on Waiting – Psalm 62 77
Papa Continues 79
Holy Spirit Teaches 82
Removal of Soul Ties 84

Broken Pieces - Mercy Triumphs 87
Battle in the Mind 92
I Am God.. 94
Prisoner of the Lord 96
The Tongue 100
Kindness... 103
The Lion's Den... 105
I Want You to Live 107
My Precious Pearl.. 111
Called to Be a Peacemaker 112
God Always Wins 116
The Parable of the Ten Virgins........................ 117
Separate Yourself... 120
I Am Amazed 122
Isaiah 31 125
I Am Your World... 130
Pearl of Great Price.. 133
Five Years Ago 137
Marriage Proposal.. 139

EPILOGUE 141
About the Author 151

Personal Letter from the Original Pearl

Greetings to you who would like an intimate relationship with the Father, Jesus, and Holy Spirit.

This is Pearl Rose.
I am blessed to practice the Presence of the Lord. I am blessed by learning to listen. Jesus tells the parable of the Pearl of Great Price in the book of Matthew. In the parable, there was a merchant in search of fine pearls. When he found one of great value, he sold all that he had and purchased it. I had been taught that Jesus was the pearl, and we are to sell our lives to Him and purchase Him.

One night, Jesus explained to me that that was not the correct interpretation. He is the merchant. After all, He owns everything and has unlimited resources of wealth. He found you. You are the valuable Pearl. You are so valuable to Him that He paid the highest price . . . His life . . . and purchased you. You are His treasure! You are Pearl. As you read the letters, realize that you are Pearl and He is speaking to you.

As I spend time in the Presence of the Trinity, I listen and write. The result is the "Letters to Pearl." I did not compose these letters...that is easily understood when you read them. I am not a genius, theologian, or scholar. I simply took dictation. I never even had to erase or start over, once I began taking dictation. You will soon recognize the Biblical Truth throughout each letter. They contain deep revelation, as well as simple concepts that are somehow deep, but simple at the same time. Only the Lord can do this. They are also written in a style that is familiar. Repetition of a major point is common in the

Bible. I personally do not repeat myself when I speak or write.

Let the reader understand that you, as a seeker of intimacy with the Trinity, are Pearl. Therefore, my earth name makes no difference. The letters were written for the Bride of Jesus...you personally, individually. Forget anyone else as you read them. They are between you and the Lover of your soul. You are Pearl.

The Lord has directed these letters be published, but I am not to make any money from them at all. I did not compose them. I do request that no one alter them in any way. They are also to be made available free of charge to all seekers of intimacy with the Lord at www.letterstopearl.com

You are free to share the information to others who may desire intimacy with the Lord. Just be careful to follow the leading of the Holy Spirit as we do not want to "cast the pearls before swine." There are many who would not receive this level of intimacy with the Lord. Do not send them or read them aloud to anyone without reassurance that this is the Lord's Will. He knows who has ears to hear.

If you are a man, do not be offended by the feminine name, Pearl. A pearl in nature is neither male or female.
May the Father, Jesus, and Holy Spirit reveal Themselves to you, heal you, teach you, and love on you in the most intimate way, as you read the letters and then spend time in His Presence.

Your Sister in Christ,
Pearl Rose

The Purpose of the Pearl Letters

The Letters to Pearl have a specific purpose, according to Holy Spirit.

Their purpose is:
1. Book One of the letters is about establishing an intimate relationship with Jesus Christ. It speaks of how much He Loves us (and Papa, of course). It heals us of our wounds and establishes truth that most of us need to hear. It is to court, woo, and reveal the truth that Jesus is our Husband and wants nothing less than serious intimacy with us. No more surface relationship. Therefore, like a man in love with a girl, He came courting, wooing, bringing kindness, healing, and inviting us to marry Him.

2. Book Two is "Come now, My Bride, sit with Me, snuggle, and I will teach you how to deal with life's hard things."

3. Book Three is about the lost sheep and how to relate to them. It ends with the Family Business.

4. Book Four is about the school of the warrior.

5. Book Five is living life to the fullest.

6. Books Six and Seven are daily devotions given in short lessons called Pearls of Wisdom.

(Note: I never planned this outline . . . I never planned anything at all! I read them right along with everyone else . . . just a little earlier. I personally think this is a great way to lay out the message. Also note the speed of the dictation . . . 350 pages in 4 ½ months . . .and that was with interruptions of being out of town or whatever. If you were to look at my handwriting you would see that the only scratched out words are those where my handwriting was so bad from being half asleep, in the dark room in the middle of the night so not to disturb my sleeping household, or misspelled words because I had to write so quickly when He dictated fast . . . or perhaps because I was excited about what I was hearing. Otherwise, no rewrites at all. There is no outline because I did not have a clue what was going to be written. I simply started with the first word, then the next, the next and then the torrent soon followed).

Finally, the Pearl who reads the letters and enters into the intimate relationship with the Trinity has been taught bit by bit how to open up and receive His Voice and Presence for herself/himself. Of course, the letters and revelation/teaching could go on forever but that is not the purpose. The point is to invite and teach each pearl to hear from the Trinity her/himself and then go on the personal journey of love, learning, and ministry united to Him. Once a Pearl gets to the end, they will be hearing from and sensing His Presence just fine . . . as long as they truly desire it, of course.

The letters are like taking a 12 month old by the hand and guiding him around until he can let go and walk on his own. First he has to figure out that his legs are truly capable of holding him up and moving. Then he has to learn lessons about balance and gravity. Then he uses props like mom or furniture to help him along. Then he gets enough confidence (faith) to let go and take off doing what he was created to do . . . walk. That is Papa's design for the letters. No more. He wants each pearl to belong to Him and depend only on Him . . . not on any letters or other person. That is one reason that I am to forever remain unknown. I am no one special. I am a grain of sand. We are also not to identify ourselves with any denomination or other organization or label. We are His and His alone. We do not depend on pastors or book authors or singers or spouses or family or friends or anyone else...we are completely attached to Papa's vine . . . abiding in only Him. All other vines are distractions at best and tares (destructive lookalike weeds) at worst.

Holy Spirit has been talking to me about intimacy with the Trinity a lot. Note: Jesus died for our sins so we can be forgiven and have eternal life. Eternal life means not separated from God when we pass into the next life. The Lord has built the New Jerusalem . . . City of God . . . beautiful, shining with His Light, streams of water flowing from Him through the city, brighter colors than we have ever known, peace, no tears, unity among the brethren, etc. Fabulous. We are not citizens of earth any longer . . . we are now citizens of Heaven.

So we have a choice. We are secure in our salvation. That is not a part of the choice. The choice is how much intimacy with the Trinity do we want. We can be . . . and already are . . . citizens in that holy city . . . OR . . . we can have that and more. We can be in the intimate Secret Place with the Trinity. Lot (Abraham's nephew) was content to be a citizen. He did leave his sinful hometown and by faith follow where God led Abraham . . .just like we do when we are saved. But that is where it ended. He was happy to be a citizen. Abraham, on the other hand, was not content to be just a citizen. He wanted intimacy. He did not care where he landed on earth, what the circumstances were . . . even to the point of sacrificing his son . . . just as long as he had intimacy with God.

Just like we have the secret place, garden of Eden, deep within our spirits, the Trinity shares a Secret Place/Garden of Eden. That is where I want to live. Give me the Secret Place of God!

It would be like this: Consider a man and a woman who get married. The man says, "Ok, honey. I will fulfill the role of my vows to you. Here is the credit card. I will provide for all your needs. Use it as you like. Here is the packet of owners' manuals for your new house, car and computer. Here, also, is a bunch of letters about how we are in a covenant (marriage contract) and how I love you. Now, if you have any problems, you can call me. Have a wonderful new life and remember that I will answer you if you call." Well, I know there are tons of people who would love and be super content with that arrangement. Not me. I want intimacy with my True Husband. I give back the credit card, house, and everything else. Rather, I say . . . "Where You go, I go. Nothing less. I will wear rags and eat from dumpsters as long as I am with You and in You. I want You . . . not Your provision. I not only want You but I want deeper and deeper intimacy with You. I want for us to possess each other (you could use the word "penetrate" but that might freak some out). I am greedy for only You!

The saddest lines in the Bible are when Jesus tells people that He has delivered or healed, "Go home," "Go in Peace," or "Pick up your bed and go home."I would say . . .okay, forget healing me, just never, never dismiss me. Let me just stay here with You forever and ever. I understand the Lord has prepared the New Jerusalem for His citizens but as for me . . . I would rather be His wife. I want to go home with my Husband when the party is over. Let everyone else enjoy the great mansions . . . I go home with my Husband to His Secret Place.

The Letters to Pearl, and all those nights/days of wonderful experiences in His Presence served to draw out my love and create an obsessive desire to have more and more intimacy with the Trinity. I love the letters and the memories of taking dictation and continuing conversations on the topics of the letters but those are just love gifts. I set down the love gifts and run into the Arms of my Lover. Nothing and no one can ever take His place. So for me . . . choosing between citizenship and intimacy is no hard thing. Give me intimacy!!

You are welcome to share this information with any Pearl. I hope it helps bring clarity and overall understanding. You all really are chosen by Papa and beautiful to Him. You will soon know that to be a fact.

Love,
Pearl

PROLOGUE

The following entries were penned in an intimate exchange over weeks between Pearl and the Lord. They were personal and specific to her and the relationship between the Lord and those in her life. They have been included for additional context for those interested in learning more about the background on how the Letters to Pearl came about.

Love - the Fullness of God   2/2013
The more time I spend in His Presence, the more Jesus and the Father flood my being with Their Love. They literally love on me over and over. They bring up wounds and heal them with Love. They bring up false beliefs, like being afraid of the Father's punishment:

There is no fear in love: but perfect love casts out fear.
I John 4:18

Because fear involves torment. But he who fears has not been made perfect in love and prove them wrong with intense love experiences. These love experiences, repeated over and over, have accomplished so much in me; forgiving the unforgivable in sincerity, forgetting the past and making all things new in my mind, giving me power to serve - even laying down everything, my own body, to one who has treated me as a hated enemy for so long. This love has captured my heart, so that I crave more and more time with Jesus and the Father. Being with Jesus, in His Presence, is all I want. ". . . and the things of earth grow strangely dim in the light of His glory and grace." All things and relationships have lost their grip on my heart - except to serve my Lord by serving others. If I never see a look of real affection for me from people again, then I am still fulfilled and very happy in this intense love from my Jesus.

Pearl -
What does it mean to be filled with the fullness of God?

. . . to know the love of Christ which passes knowledge; that you may be filled with all the fullness of God.
Ephesians 3:19

Jesus -
Well, God is Love. To be filled with My fullness is to be filled with My Love. Love is your true nature, uncorrupted. You were made of Love - of Me - in My image. So when you are filled with My fullness (My Love), you are repaired from the damage of sin and living in the world. That is why Paul, in Ephesians, and John in 1st John, urge you to experience My Love in My Presence. Once you are filled with My Fullness, you have confidence in Me and My ability to keep you, talk to you, protect you, use you, hold you, and continue to love on you. You then respond in faith, trust, confidence, and boldness. You are then equipped for My Holy Spirit to use you in ministering truth, deliverance, and healing for others without fear or intimidation. I loved on Paul for a long time while he was in My Presence, before he began his ministry. As David worshiped Me, My Presence loved on him to the point that he was happy to take great personal risks - they no longer felt like risks to him.

Pearl, don't underestimate the power of My Love for you, and the power of My Love in you for others. My Love is the Living Water. My Love is My flesh you are to eat, and My Blood you are to drink. Come to the well over and over. The more you chew My Love into your soul, the more the Holy Spirit can flow. All of My miracles were the result of My Love. Time and again I went to the well of My Father's Love, drank deeply, and then was empowered to minister. It is My Love for you, Pearl, that you have been feeling all over you. John experienced it so often that he identified himself by it.

You were healed and delivered by My Love. Then I told you to love on the one who has been like an enemy toward you, as if you were loving on Me. You obeyed and did this with the Love I gave you. As you have seen, it has broken the power of darkness and lies over this one. The whole atmosphere has changed now.

Keep coming into My Presence and drink deeply of My Love. You are comfortable with the intensity and passion now. I will open your spirit and enlarge you to receive even more of My Fullness. You are already seeing My Hand move in miracles. Pearl - you haven't seen anything yet. Remember, it is easier to heal than to forgive.

For which is easier, to say, "Your sins are forgiven you," or to say, "Arise and walk?"

Matthew 9:5

Pearl -

My experience - Jesus and the Father's Presence - is a bath in pure love, amazing, intense, passionate love that only gets stronger each day. The words They speak are Love and Life to my soul. The Truth They teach serves to open me up to more love - both to receive and to give. The out-of-the-box experiences have taught me hidden mysteries that are startling, but beautiful and full of love. So many things I never saw or did not interpret correctly in the Bible makes sense now. I will never get enough.

Jesus -

Pearl, when you obeyed My Voice and did hard things with sincerity of true love, you laid down your life for Me. I laid down My Life for you. We are laying down our lives for each other in a swirl of intense love ... two lovers who continually die for the other. There is nothing more powerful, deep, or beautiful. This is what a real marriage is to look like. The result is ultimate peace and ultimate security. You have this with Me now, Pearl - and it will continue throughout eternity.

SPOTS AND WRINKLES   2/27/13

Pearl -

. . . .that He might present her to Himself a glorious church, not having spot or wrinkle or any such thing, but that she should be holy and without blemish.

Ephesians 5:27

Jesus, I have so many spots and wrinkles left in my soul. It is hard not to be discouraged. I want to be with You in union, and in union with the Father, but I know this can't happen with all these spots and wrinkles. I felt my impatience today. I felt self-protection, self-rights, demanded to be treated better when spoken to by one person in a certain way, was too sensitive towards self, hurt when one expressed a low opinion of me, which is love of reputation and self - so much in me that has not died yet.

Jesus, I want to be beautiful to You. You desire purity in the innermost parts. I am discouraged. Pride still lives in me. I submit to the trials and pain that You have planned for me, so that this flesh can die. Thank You for the pain that has already killed off some flesh that prevented me from being close to You. I want to be closer. Therefore, I welcome more pain to kill more of me. Kill off pride and self-righteousness. I am to be empty and hidden in You - not full of myself. All glory is to go to You. All my desire is for You, Jesus. Please do whatever it takes, so I can go deeper into You and the Father. Make myself die in complete submission to Your will, trusting You.

Jesus -

My Beloved Pearl, don't be discouraged. I see through the imperfections to the pearl of great price. I Am teaching you, Pearl, each day. Just remain open . . . wide open. See My Hand behind every experience every minute of your days. I Am shaping you. Just be patient with the process. As Paul says, you are running a race and are like a farmer with his crops. The race may be long and the growing season seems to be endless, but you will eventually reach the place you long for - union with Me. Just keep looking at Me and experiencing My Love. The more you look at Me, the more you will begin to look like Me. When you look just like Me, then we will fit together perfectly and union will occur.

As for me, I will see Your face in righteousness; I shall be satisfied when I awake in Your likeness.
Psalm 17:15

So, My Precious Pearl, don't look at yourself - look at Me. I will take you through the shaping experiences and teach you, as we are communing together. Keep your eyes on Me. Remember that I love you and long for you. Your perfection is My goal. I never stop working on your behalf and to My delight. You are My reward and desire. As you lay self on the altar in all honesty, I will help you destroy it. The more your self dies, the more I fill you with Me. My beauty will fill you. My love. My purity. My humility. My trust. I always kept My eyes on the Father. You do the same. My Love will fill you.

Who can understand his errors? Cleanse me from secret faults. Keep back Your servant also from presumptuous sins; Let them not have dominion over me. Then I shall be blameless, And I shall be innocent of great transgression. Let the words of my mouth and the meditation of my heart Be acceptable in Your sight, O Lord, my strength and my Redeemer.
Psalm 19:12-14

As for today's failures, crucify the flesh by going to those people and admitting your wrongs. This will punish the flesh to death and make it easier to resist temptation next time. Come away with Me and let Me heal the wounds of discouragement.

The Father -
Pearl, take in My Love, of which you are made, and then you will be able to lose self-interest. You will then be able to look out for the interest of others. You cannot do this unless you abide in Me, drinking from My wellspring of Love. Your flesh does not have the ability to change.

Abide in Me, and I in you. As the branch cannot bear fruit of itself, unless it abides in the vine, neither can you, unless you abide in Me.

John 15:4

Only drinking My Love will enable you to let go of your interests during conversations, and identify the needs of others. Only drinking deeply from My Love will give you the desire to heal, encourage, and bless during difficult conversations. Come to My well, time and time again, so you can turn conflict into ministry. You can do nothing apart from Me, but when you continuously drink deeply of the Love I have for you, then you can leave self and all its desires behind and minister Love.

Your flesh can drown in My sea of Love.

Slow down. Don't respond so quickly. Stay connected with Me. There is no hurry to respond. Learn silence and contemplation. Do not address anything immediately. You must ask the Holy Spirit to whisper a reminder to your spirit on each occasion. Submit to Him, no matter how pressing the situation. Submit in trust and humility.

When you feel your flesh rising up, submit immediately to the Holy Spirit. Stop and listen to Him.

Pearl, read James, all of Chapter 3. (He really did put this in my head/spirit - I did not have any idea what I would find when I turned to James 3 - did not remember at all. Don't know what is better, the lesson I need or the faith-building experiences with Jesus, the Father, and the Holy Spirit I am having).

My brethren, let not many of you become teachers, knowing that we shall receive a stricter judgment. 2 For we all stumble in many things. If anyone does not stumble in word, he is a perfect man, able also to bridle the whole body.

Indeed, we put bits in horses' mouths that they may obey us, and we turn their whole body. Look also at ships; although they are so large and are driven by fierce winds, they are turned by a very small rudder wherever the pilot desires.

Even so, the tongue is a little member and boasts great things. See how great a forest a little fire kindles! And the tongue is a fire, a world of iniquity. The tongue is so set among our members that it defiles the whole body, and sets on fire the course of nature; and it is set on fire by hell.

For every kind of beast and bird, of reptile and creature of the sea, is tamed and has been tamed by mankind. But no man can tame the tongue. It is an unruly evil, full of deadly poisons. With it we bless our God and Father, and with it we curse men, who have been made in the similitude of God. Out of the some mouth proceed blessing and cursing. My brethren, these things ought not to be so. Does a spring send forth fresh water and bitter from the same opening? Can a fig tree, my brethren, bear olives, or a grapevine bear figs? Thus no spring yields both salt water and fresh.

Who is wise and understanding among you? Let him show by good conduct that his works are done in the meekness of wisdom. But if you have bitter envy and self-seeking in your hearts, do not boast and lie against the truth. This wisdom does not descend from above, but is earthly, sensual, demonic. For where envy and self-seeking exist, confusion and every evil thing are there.
But the wisdom that is from above is first pure, then peaceable, gentle, willing to yield, full of mercy and good fruits, without partiality and without hypocrisy. Now the fruit of righteousness is sown in peace by those who make peace.

James 3:1-18

Jesus -

Submit to Me and trust Me, Pearl. The more you submit to Me and trust me, the more I can use you. You have already seen how I can use you. This is only the beginning. Submit to My control. Trust Me to speak and move and lead. Don't be afraid. Step out in faith and I will take over from there. Keep your focus on Me and not on self. Self will reason away My Voice. Be sensitive to My gentle tugs; the more you trust Me, the more gentle My voice.

Pearl -

Psalm 16:1-11 means so much to me now.

Preserve me, O God, for in You I put my trust. O my soul, you have said to the Lord, "You are my Lord, My goodness is nothing apart from you." As for the saints who are on the earth, "They are the excellent ones, in whom is all my delight."

Their sorrows shall be multiplied who hasten after another god; Their drink offerings of blood I will not offer, Nor take up their names on my lips. O Lord, You are the portion of my inheritance and my cup; You maintain my lot. The lines have fallen to me in pleasant places; Yes, I have a good inheritance. I will bless the Lord who has given me counsel; My heart also instructs me in the night seasons. I have set the Lord always before me; Because He is at my right hand I shall not be moved.

Therefore my heart is glad, and my glory rejoices; My flesh also will rest in hope. For you will not leave my soul in Sheol. Nor will You allow Your Holy One to see corruption.

You will show me the path of life; In Your presence is fullness of joy; At your right hand are pleasures forevermore.

COME TO ME - NO BOUNDARIES   2/28/13 a.m.

Pearl -

As I was pressing into the Lord's Presence - into Jesus, this time there was a bright light. I knew enough of testimonials of people who died and returned to know this was Jesus. I pressed toward it when I heard, "Come to Me." I pushed ahead. Then I saw the figure of a man at the center of white rays. Nothing else around. Just intense white light with the shape of a man in the center. I came closer - ran - knew it was my Love, my Jesus.

When I got to Him, He took my breath away. Intense light and power. I know I only saw a dimmed version of the reality, since I was still in my own body. I immediately had the sense of my own grayness and a lack of glory. No shining - dull as a piece of dirt. I cried and cried. How can I come close and love on You, Jesus? How can we relate? How can I be with You? I could only fall at His feet, look at the ground, and cry. My longing for Him was intense and it became a sense of deep mourning.

"My blood will wash you, Pearl." I then felt like a wet sensation flow over my body and soul. It was thickish like chocolate syrup. I knew that I was being cleansed. I knew at once that I could never have come into Him without this cleansing. He could never take anything into Him that would dull or be a dark spot in all that light. It would mess everything up - mess up perfection of purity. Now I could walk closer and come in. The love feeling was overwhelming.

Jesus, I want to give You my Love. How can I show You and give You my love, like You have shown and given to me Yours? I wanted to love Him back - reciprocate. He said, "Die for Me, Pearl. Die to yourself.

Kill yourself. Greater love has no one than this, than to lay down one's life for his friends." Die to all rights, desires, self - interest, fairness - I knew this was what He meant. Forget books and boundaries . . . there were to be no boundaries, because boundaries are in place to preserve self, and My self had to die. Pride had to die. Pride says, "No, you cannot treat me this way, for I deserve better." Oh Jesus, help My self to die every minute.

As I recall the lives of the disciples, I realize they did not set boundaries, insist on thoughtful or civil behavior toward them. They did not fight back. They did not hire lawyers or complain about mistreatment. They accepted all events as coming from the Lover of their souls for His glory and their good. They did not quit and lick their wounds. They gave up good reputation, did not dwell on injustice, and accepted loss as a part of dying to self. Jesus died for me. Now I die for Him.

What a picture of the act of love between two people! The Stronger dies first for His love. The weaker follows His example and dies to Him. The Stronger then resurrects both of them in new oneness and light together. A complete picture of complete love. (I could never watch another chick flick - how small their love looks now!).

Jesus -
Matthew 16:25. *For whoever desires to save his life will lose it, but whoever loses his life or My sake will find it.*
This requires stepping out in surrender, trust, and faith, Pearl. You will feel your soul laying itself on the altar each time you let go and die. If you feel any sense of being wronged, bitterness, or anger, then you will know that your offering did not die on the altar. Completely let

go. Pride must die every day. There must be an element of complete abandonment to Me, a throwing up of your arms, dropping everything you were holding, and completely embracing Me instead. Don't trust Me or seek Me for fairness to be brought into your life.

Trust Me for Life to be brought into your life.
Trust Me for molding and shaping you.
Trust Me for cleansing you.
Trust Me to teach you Truth.
Trust in My complete Love for you that seeks union with you.

I want you to be in Me - in My embrace - so that is what I Am preparing for you - no spot or wrinkle. You are becoming a beautiful bride for Me, more beautiful with each death of self and step of trust. So attractive to Me, I can hardly contain Myself like an eager bridegroom. I love you, Pearl. Trust Me as I lead you through this process.

Pearl, what you are experiencing in My Presence is My Love nourishing you. You are My wife. As your Husband, I Am nourishing you. It is pleasurable, sweet wine. Drink deeply, Pearl. Come again and again. Feed from Me. You are flesh of My flesh, bone of My bone.

"So husbands ought to love their own wives as their own bodies; he who loves his wife loves himself. For no one ever hated his own flesh, but nourishes and cherishes it, just as the Lord does the church" – you, Pearl.

For we are members of His body, of His flesh and of His bones.

PURIFIED 2/28/13 p.m.

Little Pearl,
Read Leviticus chapter 21. This chapter describes some of the requirements for holiness for My priests. Priests come near to Me; they serve Me personally. They had interactions with Me. They came into My Presence. If they came into My Presence after defiling themselves, they would immediately be destroyed.

Those requirements were not meant to be restrictions from a distant cold and angry God, as some think. No, those requirements were a gift of Mercy. Those who misunderstood, do so because they do not know Me. If I Am complete holiness, I Am complete purity... I Am pure fire. Therefore, anyone with any hint of impurity or imperfection, who came into My Presence, would be destroyed by My substance. Imperfection cannot exist near Me. It is impossible. This is why I called you to separate yourself from the world. This is why I had to send a part of Myself, My purity in the form of My Son, to die for you. I want you to be near Me at all times, Pearl.

Notice that the priests could not marry an impure wife. Those who were divorced or were not virgins when they married were not eligible to become wives of priests. Because I made a special covenant with you, Little Pearl, Jesus can now be your Priest and Husband. He is your High Priest Who prays for you and offered Himself as a Sacrifice for you. He is your Husband Who covers you, teaches you, shapes you into His own image, so that you can come near to Me without being destroyed. Now you do not need to be afraid of My fire or My holiness. You have returned to your original soul - state. You can now approach My throne as a cleansed bride of

My Son; a bride who is without spot or wrinkle or anything that represents imperfection. Don't be afraid of My Enormity and Power. Don't be afraid of My Blinding Light. For you, Little Pearl, My Enormity, Power, and Light mean the inexhaustible supply, force, and beauty of My Love for you. Not so for those who reject a real relationship with Jesus. They do have reason to fear. To them, I Am enormous, powerful, and blinding alone. They cannot experience My Love, while rejecting My Provision for cleansing. But you, Little Pearl, I want to come running to Me and enjoy the Enormity, the Power, and Light of My Love for you. Enjoy the Holiness that your Priest and Husband provide you. Be secure in Our Love and your holiness. Bask in My Love, like a child enjoys playing with his good father.

Enjoy the fact that, as your Husband, He also purifies you and makes you completely holy. You do not need to be protected from My Presence any longer. Now I eagerly cry out to you, "Come to Me, My Pearl! Come into My Presence; you not only will survive being in My Presence, you will THRIVE in My Presence. You will be more full of life than you thought possible. You will feel like you are breathing and seeing for the first time. You will know Pure Love and security for the first time ever. Swim in the river of My Love, Little Pearl. Yes, that is possible while you are still on Earth. Just begin to focus on Me in your spirit. You are now holy. The more time you spend with Me, the more you will embrace your holiness, and the less enticing sin will be to you. Draw near to Me, Little Pearl, without fear - thanks to your Priest - Husband. I will draw near to you. Come for the hug of your life!

WASHED   2/28/13 p.m.

Jesus -

Pearl, you are My bride. My bride must be pure ... pure in mind, body, and soul. Purity comes from washing in the Word. I Am the Word. Therefore, come to Me to wash you and make you pure. I wash you in My blood. I wash you in My Love. I wash you in My Presence. As long as you remain on Earth and in your current body, you will need to come to Me continuously to be washed. Come freely without hesitation. Come often. There is no condemnation - just cleansing. This is how you purify your heart - by coming to Me. This purification or cleansing process will not only cleanse you from all unrighteousness, but it will also reconnect you with My Love. Your mind will be renewed. Your wounds healed. Truth restored. Love confirmed. Faith built. Keep coming to My well of Living Water. It is My Love for you and it will never run dry.

The Lord has His way in the whirlwind and in the storm, and the clouds are the dust of His feet.
                                                    Nahum 1:3

Don't resist the coming storms. Don't resent them or turn away. I Am in the storm. I Am in the tragedy and the pain. I can be found in the confusion and loss. The heartache is Me . . . calling you to yourself. The storm reminds you of who you are - a weak, dependent creature made of dust. Even though you try, you can do nothing apart from Me. Your own wisdom is foolishness. Your own strength gives way like rotten wood. Your joy won't last and your burdens will become overbearing to the breaking point.

Seek the Lord while He may be found. Seek Me in the storm. Seek Me in the pain and confusion. Attach yourself to the hem of My garment. I will stop the issue of blood that is flowing from your wounds. Seek Me while I can be found. The day will come when you seek Me and cannot find Me. Now is the time.

The storm may rage, but in the eye of the storm is My Presence. In the eye of the storm is My Peace. Wait, in trust and simple faith, for the eye of the storm to pass over you. If you refuse to submit and wait, you will get lost in the storm. Do not resent the storm. It is for your good - to bring you into My Presence. Thank Me for the storm and the eye of the storm will remain on you. Do not be bitter about the pain and loss. Rest in the eye of the storm and submit to My rule. There you will be healed and joy will return. Trust Me and submit. I Love you with an everlasting love. It is My Love that sent the storm. It is My Love that won't let you go on longer without Me.

Pearl -

I have the impression that was for many people today. I hope it reaches them and delivers them. I went through a season like that and could have greatly benefitted by this message.

Jesus -

To be understood is one of man's greatest needs. It is second to the desire to be loved. I understand. There is nothing about you that I cannot understand or relate to. Pain and sorrow assailed Me. Joyful fellowship and delight in loved ones I also understand. I know what guilt and shame does to the heart. Fear, confusion - I bore these on the cross. I understand all. That is why I can heal your broken heart and mend your wounds. So don't stop coming to Me. Soak in My Love. Listen to Me as I teach you. Follow Me in earnestly praying, *"Father, forgive them for they know not what they do."*

Luke 23:34

Cast all your cares on Me for I care for you. Be still and know that I Am God. Isaiah 46:4 Even to your old age, I Am He. And even to gray hairs I will carry you!

I Peter 5:7

BEAR ONE ANOTHER'S BURDEN   3/1/13

Jesus -

Pearl, bear with that one's sin. *Bear one another's burdens and so fulfill the law of Christ* (Galatians 6:2). Don't expect love and righteousness from others. Do expect Me to be working in their lives, just like I Am working in yours. You felt your own flesh rise up in judgment and self-righteousness. Don't be discouraged by your own propensity for sin either. *I will perfect that which concerns you* (Ps 138:8). You immediately came to Me with your sin and the offense of the other one. That is good. I heal and forgive. Now you are free to love and minister My grace to the other. Do not worry about whether the other sees their sin. That is My business, not yours.

I bore the burden of your sin. When you bear the burden of another's sin toward you, you are following in My footsteps, imitating Me. You are sharing in My suffering. You are being conformed into My image. This means we will have greater intimacy since we will be more alike - we will fit together better and better - like putting the middle puzzle piece in a complete puzzle.

Pearl, do you realize that I not only suffered in My body for your sin, but I also poured out My very soul, even to the point of death?

Because He poured out His soul unto death, And He was numbered with the transgressors, And He bore the sin of many, and made intercession for the transgressor.
Isaiah 53:12

I understand how the sin of others causes pain to your soul. I understand how your own sin causes pain to your own soul. Bear or carry the sin of others, as I bore your sin. Let Me make you more like Me, and the pleasure of our nearness will last forever. Where there is sin, there is grace enough.

You will cast all our sins into the depths of the sea.
Micah 7:19

I will feed and nourish you, Pearl, but you must come to Me without bitterness or resentment in your heart toward anyone. I will expose the resentment. You pay attention and recognize it for what it is. You then must begin the dying - to - yourself process again. Forgive through the power of My Spirit. Push through the feelings until you have released all sense of injustice, unfairness, unkindness, and wrongness. Trust Me. As you give up your rights, you will die. I will then resurrect new life in your spirit. Old things will be gone and your heart will be made new. You and I will go through this process over and over, as I am making you to be My bride that is without spot or wrinkle. So, each incident, feeling of anger, and self-pity serve to begin this death - to - life process again. You will continue to die for Me over and over, My beautiful Pearl.

Pearl, you died for Me today, three times. Each time you die to yourself for Me, it is a sweet-smelling sacrifice to Me, and newness of life springs up in you. You open the doors for My Spirit to come in power when you die for Me. My Spirit can freely work miracles in, through, and around you, when you die for Me.

Each death of your flesh creates more room for Me in you. You are being conformed to My image. You are being transformed. You are beautiful to Me. With each painful death of self comes My healing and filling. Your faith and trust in Me is growing. Without faith you cannot please Me (Hebrews 11:6).

Pearl, I am pleased - thrilled with you. I will always be there each time you die for Me. Then I will always heal you and breathe more life and more of My Presence into you. Keep coming to Me for every little thing. You are not meant to do anything on your own. Yes, you feel more needy now than ever, but that is because you are closer to Me and recognizing your need. You do not try My patience - I love to meet every need. That is My plan for us. Draw from Me. Drink deeply of My Love. Gather My peace. This is My delight.

Book One

PARABLE OF THE TEN LEPERS　　　　3/8/13

Pearl -
While driving on a long trip, I asked Jesus, "Please teach me more. I can't have my Bible in front of me, but I do have plenty of time. I can listen."

Jesus -
Immediately He said, "In the story of the ten lepers, I healed all ten while they were on their way to show themselves to the priests. Only one came back to thank Me, when they discovered their leprosy was gone. Only one was grateful and turned around to find Me. He not only thanked Me, but he fell down at My feet.

I asked, "Jesus, what were the nine thinking? Why not run back and say 'Thank you!'?"

Jesus -
Pride leads men to entitlement. Pride says, 'I deserve this. Of course this should happen. It is only right.' The one who returned was a Samaritan. He had no sense of entitlement. He realized his sinful state and recognized this as a gift of undeserved love. He didn't just say thanks. He cried in a loud voice. He was not concerned about what the onlookers thought. His sinful needy soul came in contact with Love and understanding. He recognized the truth about himself and loved My mercy. The others never saw the truth about themselves. They were Jews who simply had the misfortune of this disease. Of course, it was only right that they should be healed. They did everything right, were from good families in the Jewish traditions.

Pride is blinding, Pearl. Pride says, 'My wife should do such and such, because, after all, she is my wife and I

deserve this. My parents should give me such and such, because I deserve it. My family should treat me with kindness, because I serve them well and give them love and kindness. They should see how much I love them and love me back.' Pride expects gifts and service. Pride demands a return of favors and the same or higher level of service. Pride has self-centered expectations. No one is grateful for what they feel is rightfully theirs to begin with. Humility focuses on Me, Pearl, and your constant state of dependency on Me. You can do nothing without Me. Without Me, you only deserve separation from Me.
I asked, "So what can be done about the nine to help them see?"

He said, "I healed the nine because, while they were yet sinners, I Loved them and was going to die for them. The power of Love, to a hardened heart - hardened by pride and jealousy - is like a battering ram. You must ram the door with Love over and over again, and eventually the door will give way. Pearl, keep using the power of My Love on those hard, blind, and prideful hearts in your life. Love them often. You have seen how blind they are to your services and gifts for them. Pride does that. It does not see or acknowledge acts of love. Don't be discouraged. Love always wins. Come to Me continually for a refill of My Presence and Love. You can't give love you don't have. Come soak in My Love until you are overflowing. Then their pride, demands, and anger won't be intimidating. You will be like a battering ram to their hearts. Miracles will begin. Just wait and watch."

"Pearl, do you feel that feeling of fulfillment and joy?"

"Yes, Jesus. It is Your Presence in me."

"Pearl, you have had a measure of this feeling with those in your life I gave you. Your children brought you joy and fulfillment. Being with certain people fulfilled you. Be careful. When you are fulfilled by someone other than Me, the you are in danger. This relationship might become a soul-tie or idolatry for you. Back away and come to Me. Reaffirm My place in your heart. Choose again - Me or that relationship. I Am jealous for you, Pearl. I won't share you with anyone. There are only two allowed in our world, Pearl - you and Me. My Love for you is intense and all-consuming. You are Mine and Mine alone."

Jesus, there is something about You being jealous for me that is hugely attractive, appealing, wonderful, and makes me crazy in Love with You! I choose You! Take every one else away. I choose You!

Another lesson for me:
Pearl, in the account of the paralyzed man who was let down through the roof, the Pharisees had asked Me a question. I had forgiven the man of his sins and the Pharisees asked, "Who can forgive sins but God alone?"
I answered their question by demonstrating My authority. I asked them a question, "Which is easier, to forgive or to heal?" The Pharisees did not answer Me, because they had never forgiven or healed anyone. They honestly did not know the answer. I know. It is easier to heal a sick body or do anything else than it is to forgive someone who has sinned against you.

Think about it, Pearl. What are very difficult things to do for people? Go to the dentist? Go back to school? Speak in public? Plan a funeral? Learn a new language? What is difficult for you? Now think of a person who has wronged, wounded, and hurt you. Perhaps they feel justified in their actions and do not want forgiveness. Now which is easier - to do that difficult thing, or to forgive that person to the point of looking at them without remembering their sin, being happy to serve them, talk with them, cheer them, console them, and be affectionate toward them?

Only My Holy Spirit can give you the power to forgive. You cannot do this on your own. In the realm of My Kingdom, forgiveness is tremendous power on display. This power you can only receive by spending time with Me and submitting to My will. It is truly supernatural, miraculous power. It takes much more power to forgive than to heal. I want you to do both.

Come to Me in the simplicity of a little child. If you are self-conscious, then confess your pride. Desire to kill pride. Ask Me. Mourn over your pride, for it prevents you from awareness of Me. We cannot have real fellowship where there is pride.

Strip all earth desires from your heart. Desire only Me. Sit still before Me with only your need and desire for Me, like a child or simple-hearted person. Be confident in My desire to be with you. I died so that all barriers between us would be torn down. It was for the purpose of intimacy with you that I died. It is My greatest desire. The Father, Holy Spirit, and I enjoy continual intimate and intense relations with Each Other and in Each Other. We desire the same with you. That is what you were created for - no other higher purpose than to be in union and fellowship with Us. So approach My Presence in confidence that this is in My perfect Will. Yes, I will "show up." Be still and know that I AM God. I AM God and I speak. I Love you, My child, and I want fellowship with you. Forget the past. Forget the current events and worries. Just enter into the Secret Place with Me.

David was a man after My own heart. That is usually interpreted as Me having a greater Love for him. I do Love David, but there is much more. Notice the word, "after." It means, to pursue. David pursued me. During his life, David never stopped seeking Me. During good times he sought My presence. During tragedy he sought my Presence. He wrote songs to allow music to usher him into My Presence. When he sinned, he begged Me not to take My Presence from him, because he loved it so much. David sought Me with all his heart - and he found Me.

Be still in your soul before Me. Keep the eyes of your soul on Me in the same way Stephen kept his eyes on Mine. Open your soul ears to My voice. You were made to hear My Voice. I Am not a god who is distant - I Am closer than your breath. Your body is My temple. I choose to live in you for the purpose of fellowshipping with you on the most intimate level. Just seek Me. My Kingdom is within you. You invited Me in. Now let's commune together. You and I, together, forever.
That has always been the Great Plan.

BY THE WILL OF GOD   3/9/13

Pearl -
Paul, an apostle of Jesus Christ, by the will of God . . .
II Timothy 1:1

By the will of God. By the will of God. By the will of God. Jesus, as I meditate on these five words, the desire for Your Will begins to consume me. Your Presence and Will are so pleasurable and delightful that I want nothing else all day. I want Your Will to be done in me and through me so badly, it feels obsessive. I am craving Your Will.

To submit to Your will is a passionate desire. Delight does not describe it. Ecstasy is a better description. Dying for You becomes a desire that is above all others. Dying to myself or dying physically - it does not matter - I want both. May Your Kingdom come and Your Will be done in me and through me. Serving You is my joy and passion. I crave for Your will to be done in me. "By the Will of God . . . "Never had this deep desire before - love it!

And when Jesus had cried out with a loud voice, He said, "Father, into Your hands I commit My spirit." Having said this, He breathed His last.

Luke 23:46

Into Your hand I commit my spirit. You have redeemed me, O Lord God of truth.

Psalm 31:5

Jesus -
Pearl, try not to dwell on the trials, persecutions, unkindness, injustice, and wrongs of others. When you

face hardship of any kind, meditate on the prayer I prayed while suffering, "Father, into Your hands I commit My spirit." Then focus on giving your spirit completely over to Me. Don't let your mind race with thoughts about what is happening around and to you. Rather, withdraw from your Mind, and focus on releasing your spirit to Me. When you trust Me with your spirit, I become both a refuge and a shield. I protect you from fear by filling your spirit with My Love, from self-pity by your act of losing your life, from unforgiveness by delivering you from expectations of others. Your spirit will be fulfilled when you give it to Me during suffering. Commit your spirit to Me during pain, disappointment, frustration, and loss. Trust Me. Follow My example.

Pearl, there is nothing more wonderful than the fellowship between the Trinity - Father, Son, and Holy Spirit. How precious are you to Us, Pearl? How much do We want you with Us? You are so wanted, loved, longed-for, that We were willing to do the most painful and difficult thing ever done - break the fellowship of the Trinity. We broke fellowship while Jesus was on the cross, so that He could bring you into Our Fellowship. Then, as John said in First John 1, Our joy could be complete because you, Pearl, are now in Our Fellowship. Welcome, Precious Pearl, to Our Fellowship.

Pearl, read: Acts 16:1-2 *Then he came to Derbe and Lystra. And behold, a certain disciple was there, named Timothy, the son of a certain Jewish woman who believed, but his father was Greek. He was well spoken of by the brethren who were at Lystra and Iconium.*

Then read: 2 Timothy 1:5 *When I call to remembrance the genuine faith that is in you, which dwelt first in your grandmother Lois and your mother Eunice, and I am persuaded is in you also.*

Notice that Timothy came from an unequally yoked family. His mother was a believer, but not his father. There were two different views about virtually everything in that home. The father was the head of the household, so he was dominant. Eunice, Timothy's mother, was Mine. In cultural and physical reality, Eunice was weak and had no authority or leadership. Decisions were not hers to make. She had no control over their lives, including the lives and beliefs of her children. She had to leave everything in My hands. This put her in a position of great strength. Notice that she did not divorce her unbelieving husband.

This allowed Timothy to see the two contrasting views and lifestyles all the way through his youth and into his adulthood. Every day he received a lesson about Me and My strength for those who trust Me. Every day he saw his mother's faith take her through difficult circumstances without knowing what the future held, or whether or not remaining with this man would be "worth it." Timothy watched My provision for her and became convinced that hers was the truth. He gave himself so fully to Me that other believers noticed. Because of this believing woman, who presented a great contrast lesson of two choices to her children, I was able to do great work and reach many hearts. The ripple effect changed the world. This would not have happened, if Eunice had given up and walked away from the marriage.

Trust Me. I will sustain you through any and every hardship. Don't project your fears into the future. Don't make decisions based on your future predictions. I give manna for today - one day at a time. In My Presence is joy forevermore. Therefore, you can be assured that, as long as you remain with Me, in My Presence, your future will be filled with joy. Just trust Me. I love you dearly and completely. Your life will be fulfilling and joyous in Me. No need to worry about the circumstances. Where there is sin, there is grace. That not only means grace for your sin, but also grace for you to bear with the sins of others. My grace is sufficient for you in every situation. My joy is available for you and more than enough to carry you through. Just remain in intimacy with Me. Maintain your awareness of My Presence, especially during the difficult interactions.

Come to Me for healing afterwards and sit in My Presence, soaking up My Love, drinking My Living Water, while I heal you and help you to forgive and love. Each incident you go through will bring you deeper into Me. You will learn to die to yourself over and over, forgive the "unforgivable," and love the "unlovable." You will be transformed into My image, as your own flesh dies. The result will be more and more intimacy with Me. This is the walking on water. This is walking above circumstances. This is walking in the Kingdom with Me. Eunice endured with Me. Therefore, Timothy made a choice between the two views. Then I used him to be a part of changing the world.

Come away with Me, My Love. Let's walk this journey together.

LET ME BUILD YOUR HOUSE   3/9/13

Unless the Lord builds the house, they labor in vain.
Psalms 127:1

Let Me build the house of your life. Trust Me in a much deeper way than before. Walk on water with Me. Don't look back at the pain, sin, and chaos of the past. Don't use past experiences to try to interpret the present or predict the future. Relax, let go, and live in the moment with Me. The more you are aware of My Presence, the less you will be concerned about your circumstances. Talk to Me about your life. Then be quiet in My Presence and listen to Me.

Notice how I will gradually steer the conversation away from the circumstances to the topic of your heart and the weaknesses therein, which keep you in turmoil about the circumstances. We will together navigate the points of flesh that must be observed, and then removed. Then I will bring freedom to work and rest in peace. This is how I will build the house of your life. This house will then be a place of refuge, truth, and healing for others. Your life is not meant for you to build alone, or even with another person. Your life is to be built by Me - and all that is not built by Me will be burned. It is a waste of time and effort. Relinquish control. Trust Me. Let go. We will walk together moment by moment if you trust Me, abide in My Presence, and submit to Me. Your life will then become a beautiful temple for Me. If I am lifted up in the temple, I will draw others to Me.

Don't mistake My Presence. In My Presence is joy, healing, love, peace, and truth. My sheep will know My Voice. Don't be fooled by a counterfeit. Your flesh cannot produce My Presence. The evil one will not produce the fruit of the Spirit in you. My Presence will be easy for you to recognize, just like a father is recognized by the child living under his care. Trust Me. I can keep you, just trust Me.

I AM YOUR NEW REALITY　　　　　3/10/13

Pearl, I Am your new reality now. I Am Newness of Life - your new life. Behold I make all things new. Your old reality is gone. My Presence is your life now. Your life is hidden in Me. It is no longer you who live in your life, but Me. The more you surrender to Me, the more I live in and through you. Each day you die to your will and each day I live more fully in you. Look to Me constantly. Seek My Will and My Voice constantly. Focus on things "above," and not things below. Detach from earthly things. Do not get entangled by the things of this world. As for other people, the more you detach, the less you depend on their love, the more you are free to serve and love them through Me. Let Me love them, while you just love Me. I Love you completely, Pearl. Focus on My Love constantly. Focus on My Presence constantly. Stay "in the zone," as you call it. Submit to My authority. I have been given all authority by My Father. Submit and be comforted by My authority. Seek refuge under My authority. It is a shelter for you.

If you seek her as silver, And search for her as for hidden treasures; Then you will understand the fear of the Lord, And find the knowledge of God. For the Lord gives wisdom; From His mouth come knowledge and understanding; He stores up sound wisdom for the upright; He is a shield to those who walk uprightly; He guards the paths of justice, And preserves the way of His saints.

　　　　　　　　　　　　　　　　　　　Prov. 2:4-8

Let your spirit remain in My Spirit constantly. That is how you "walk in the Spirit." Your spirit in union with My Spirit is My Will for you. When your spirit is one with Mine, you will not "fulfill the lust of the flesh," or become entangled in the things of earth, because I will be the focus of your desire. Enjoy My Authority over you. Enjoy submitting to Me. Yes, submission to My Will is enjoyable for you. It is comforting. It is security. Old things have passed away for you, Pearl. I Am your new world, your new reality.

Behold I stand at the door and knock. If anyone hears My voice and opens the door, I will come in to him and dine with him and he with Me.

Rev. 3:20

Pearl, even though We are married, I will continually knock at the door of your heart. I will court you and woo you and seek to win your heart over and over. Even though you have given yourself to Me, I will never stop courting you, as if for the first time. You will always be a Bride to Me - not a long-married wife, but a newly-married bride. I will seek to please you. Our relationship will always be fresh. There will always be more to explore, experience, and feed upon.

Yes, you asked what We will be dining upon - the answer is Our Love. Our Love for each other is Our food. I will seek to win more and more of your love. I pleasure you and you pleasure Me. How do you pleasure Me? By your trust in Me. By your acceptance of My invitations. By your desiring My Presence. By your willingness to die to yourself for Me. By your submission to Me. By your seeking Me. By your waiting for Me. By your responding to My Love. By your enjoyment of My Presence, the pleasure it brings. The Union of Our Spirits brings great pleasure to Me as well. Let's dine together, you and Me. Alone. Just us. No one else allowed. No distractions. No other thoughts in your mind. Come into your spirit and meet with Me. There I will court you, dine with you, and be your Husband. Shut the door after you have opened it to Me. No one else is allowed to come in. I am eager, Pearl.

Song of Solomon:

6:2 *My beloved has gone to his garden, To the beds of spices, To feed his flock in the gardens, And to gather lilies.*

7:6 *How fair and how pleasant you are, O love, with your delights!*

5:1 *I have come to my garden, my sister, my spouse; I have gathered my myrrh with my spice; I have eaten my honeycomb with my honey; I have drunk my wine with my milk*

4:12 *A garden enclosed Is my sister, my spouse. A spring shut up, A fountain sealed.*

4:9 *You have ravished my heart, My sister, my spouse; You have ravished my heart With one look of your eyes, With one link of your necklace.*

7:10 *I am my beloved's, and his desire is toward me.*

7:13 *The mandrakes give off a fragrance, And at our gates are pleasant fruits, All manner, new and old, Which I have laid up for you, my beloved.*

1:2 *Let him kiss me with the kisses of his mouth - For your love is better than wine.*

YOU DIED FOR ME TODAY　　　　　　　3/11/13

Jesus -

Pearl, you died for Me again today. Go read Psalm 116 (I had no idea what I would find there).

I love the Lord because He has heard My voice and my supplications. Because He has inclined His ear to me, Therefore, I will call upon Him as long as I love. The pains of death surrounded me, And the pangs of Sheol laid hold of me; I found trouble and sorrow. Then I called upon the name of the Lord: "O Lord, I implore You, deliver my soul!" Gracious is the Lord, and righteous; Yes, our God is merciful. The Lord preserves the simple; I was brought low, and He saved me. Return to your rest, O my soul, For the Lord has dealt bountifully with you. For You have delivered my soul from death, My eyes from tears, and my feet from falling. I will walk before the Lord In the land of the living. I believed, therefore I spoke, "I am greatly afflicted." I said in my haste, "All men are liars." What shall I render to the Lord For all His benefits toward me? I will take up the cup of salvation, And call upon the name of the Lord. I will pay my vows to the Lord now in the presence of all His people. Precious in the sight of the Lord is the death of His saints.

Psalm 116:1-15

Pearl, of course I noticed (He responded to my tears). You knew it was going to happen and turned yourself over to Me. That is why it was a beautiful offering on the altar - a sweet - smelling offering. Each time you die for Me, I Am intoxicated with the sweet fragrance and by My Love for you. We are dying together, you and I, over and over again. Our Love is then being renewed in new life, ever growing more powerful. Come to the

Father and Me now, and We will heal you. We will always heal and renew you when you die. There will be many more deaths for you before your final sacrifice. We will do this together, Pearl. Each time you die for Me, you become more and more beautiful to Me. My beautiful bride!

HIS PRESENCE   3/13/13

The Father —

Little Pearl, the accuser of the brethren, your enemy, is constantly seeking to condemn you. When you are out among people, there is pollution. You are affected by the pollution. Come to Me to cleanse you from all unrighteousness and soul-wounds. Remember that I do not condemn you. I wash you. Therefore, do not fear. Your fear will cause you not to be aware of My Presence and Love. Come to Me in trust. Trust in My Love for you. If I discipline you, I will do it in love. I will not press a heavy load of guilt upon you. I will gently convict you. If I chasten you, then come to Me for love and healing, like a parent who disciplines and then hugs their child.

When you go into a crowd or with friends and converse with them, remain conscious of My Presence. My Presence will protect your heart. My Presence will guard your mouth. If you are not aware of Me, go to a private place and focus on Me in your spirit, then return, guided by My Spirit. Walk in My Spirit and you won't fulfill the lusts of your flesh. My Presence will protect you from the world and also from your own flesh. Remain in Me, cleansed by My Love. Remain pure by My Love. Avoid confusion by My Love. If you stumble or stray, return to My Love. I will restore you and nourish you back to health and life every single time. Feed on My faithfulness, depend on My loving kindness, enter into My Loving Presence.

Who can understand his errors? Cleanse me from secret faults. Keep back Your servant also from presumptuous sins; Let them not have dominion over me. Then I shall be blameless, And I shall be innocent of great transgression. Let the words of my mouth and the meditation of my heart be acceptable in Your sight, O Lord, my strength and my Redeemer.

Psalm 19:12-14

Little Pearl, what you are feeling is My rest. You have entered into My rest. Those waves of peace flowing over you are My Breath of Love. My Love and peace are flowing over and into you. They are healing and teaching you. This is another side to My Love. You experienced My nourishing Love yesterday. Now you are experiencing rest and peace-giving Love. Your soul is soaking up My Love.

Pearl - I think my house could burn down and I would not care at all. All cares are gone - drowned in these waves of peace and love that are rolling over and over me. It is the most incredible massage ever - a massage both inside and out, head to feet, back and forth. I sleep a little, still aware of it, then wake feeling the rolling waves, then sleep, then wake, back and forth, over and over again. I hated to sit up, but Papa said to write. It is almost 1:00 A.M., but I feel completely refreshed, as if I just had a full night's sleep. Emotionally I have nothing but peace and gratitude. How do I deserve this? I don't. How can I repay? I can't. I can only marvel, worship, and thank my Papa.

In the night His song shall be with me, and my prayer unto the God of my life.

Psalm 42:8b

He gives power to the weak, And to those who have no might He increases strength. Even the youths shall faint and be weary, And the young men shall utterly fall. But those who wait on the Lord Shall renew their strength;

They shall mount up with wings like eagles, They shall run and not be weary, They shall walk and not faint.
Isaiah 40:29-31

The earth was without form, and void; and darkness was on the face of the deep. And the Spirit of God was hovering over the face of the waters.
Genesis 1:2

For we who have believed do enter that rest, as He has said: So I swore in My wrath, "They shall not enter My rest."11 Let us therefore be diligent to enter that rest, lest anyone fall according to the same example of disobedience.
Hebrews 4:3, 11

Father –
Little Pearl, I Am your Protector. I Love you. You are My daughter. I guard you and keep you hidden in My Hand. Because My Love for you is complete; no weapon formed against you can prosper. There is no greater force than My Love for you. Let all your fears and insecurities melt away as you experience My Love. I Am surrounding you. I Am permeating you. Nothing and no one can make Me let go of you or separate Me from you. Relax into My Love. I will protect you, no matter what the circumstances. I may lead you into rough waters, but I will always protect you. Trust Me.

My Little Pearl, My heart yearns after you. Little Pearl, the more you experience Me, the more you love Me. The more you love Me, the more I can protect you, because you will stay under the shelter of My wings. Those who do not know Me do not stay under My shelter. Listen to My gentle convictions of sin. This is protection for you.

Lord, who may abide in Your tabernacle? Who may dwell in Your holy hill? He who walks uprightly, and works righteousness, and speaks the truth in his hear; He who does not backbite with his tongue, nor does evil to his neighbor, nor does he take up a reproach against his friend; In whose eyes a vile person is despised, but he honors those who fear the Lord; He who swears to his own hurt and does not change; He who does not put out his money at usury, nor does he take a bribe against the innocent. He who does these things shall never be moved.

Psalm 15

Catch us the foxes, the little foxes that spoil the vines, for our vines have tender grapes.

Song of Solomon 2:15

Little Pearl, the answer to your question is curds and honey . . . curds (milk) from My breast and honey from Jesus' mouth. Isaiah 7:15 *Curds and honey He shall eat, that He may know to refuse the evil and choose the good.* "The land of milk and honey." This is a picture of Me nourishing My babies or loved ones (you) with My own milk, and Jesus feeding them with the sweetness of the Word (Himself) from His own mouth. This is how I raise My own children. When they are raised on My breast milk and Jesus' honey, they know to refuse evil and choose good. They have the strength to refuse evil and to desire for good. Feeding on Me and from Jesus is abiding in My Vine. Strength and wisdom flow into you, mixed with desire for more of Me. This combination changes you into more of My image, protects you, nourishes you, strengthens you, and pleasures you. Come and take your nourishment from Me. I will hold you and Love on you, while you drink in My milk and Love.

Little Pearl, the more you obey My still small Voice and gentle nudgings, trusting Me rather than logic, perceptions, or your own feelings, then the more We can travel the high places together. You know what your assignment is. Jesus learned obedience through suffering. I know it is hard, but that is why you need Me to accomplish your task. Don't ignore those impressions of seemingly small, but difficult things - like hugging the one who causes you pain, serving and giving compassionate support to the one who is being used to oppress you. Remember to always pray as Jesus did, *"Father, forgive them for they know not what they do." Forgive, serve, and trust Me for the rest.* There is great power in obedience. You will sense more and more of My Presence as you obey.

END OF PROLOGUE

ABANDON ALL FOR ME 3/17/13

Little Pearl, when I give you happy blessings, you recognize them as coming from Me and thank Me. What if I give you painful blessings? Now you are being made to give up something you love. Don't be tempted to feel the injustice. Don't resent the one being used to do this. Abandon everything to Me. I Am jealous over you. I want you to depend on Me and Me alone. Seasons of aloneness are My way of ensuring that you belong to Me alone. I will be your Teacher, fellowship, and joy. I will fulfill you. Are you willing to abandon all for Me? Or do you suppose that the Scripture is speaking to no purpose that says, The Spirit Whom He has caused to dwell in us yearns over us - and He yearns for the Spirit [to be welcome] - with a jealous love (James 4:5 Amplified)?

Little Pearl, as you serve and lay your life down for another, that one will begin to persecute you less and depend upon you more. Serve and show love. This softens hearts and melts resentment. Guard your own heart against resentment. There is power in loving your enemy. As people rely upon you more, trust you more, and soften toward you, I will use you to lead them to Me. Persevere. Do not grow weary or discouraged. Don't give in to self-pity, for that is loving yourself. Love Me alone. Lose yourself. Lose your life. The more you serve Me in pain, the less pain you will have, as your love for Me grows. Our relationship will grow richer, deeper, and more beautiful. Keep your eyes on Me alone.

HOLY SPIRIT SPEAKS   3/18/13 p.m.

Holy Spirit - My Friend Pearl,
I Am the Holy Spirit and I Am your Friend. A comforter and helper is a companion. A friend is one who speaks truth and gives wise counsel. A friend strengthens and gives courage to the discouraged and weak. I hover over you, as I hovered over the waters. You would not be in the Father's and Jesus' Presence, if not for Me as your channel. I will always guide you into Their Presence. I Am the Power of God and the Light in your soul. I Am the One Who conforms you into the image of Jesus. I teach you deep in your spirit the truth that you seek. I will never leave you, because Jesus gave Me to you as a gift of Love. He treasures Me and knew that you would treasure Me also.

Notice, Pearl, how Jesus protected Me from the Pharisees, when He said that if any sins against Me, they would not be forgiven. Jesus and the Father love Me, and They love you, and I love you. As you come to know Me more, you will love Me intimately, just like you love the Father and Jesus. Then Our circle of Love will be complete. You are complete, Pearl. You have a Father, Papa, a Husband, Jesus, and a Friend, Me. Father, Husband, Friend - We complete you and fill all the longings of your soul.

RESTORING HIS IMAGE 3/19/13

God said, "Let Us make mankind in Our image, after Our likeness . . . " So God created man in His own image, in the image and likeness of God He created him; male and female He created them.

Genesis 1:26-27

When God created man, He made him in the likeness of God. He created them male and female and blessed them.

Genesis 5:1, 2

Little Pearl, it is My desire to restore you to My image. For you to look just like Me was My original design. What is My image? I Am Love. Pure Love. I Am joy and peace. Jesus is the exact representation of My image. His love is completely reflected in His life, death, and resurrection. There is nothing self-centered in Him. He is purely motivated by love, willingly obedient, completely trusting My Will, seeking only My pleasure, desiring to restore fellowship with man. When you study Jesus, talk with Jesus, and experience Jesus, you are seeing a perfect image of Me.

Man is so marred by sin that it is very difficult to find My image in him at all. I Am restoring you to My image. That is My desire for you, Little Pearl. How? Who you listen to, observe, identify with, admire, and spend time with is who you will eventually look like. A rebellious teen will eventually look just like his delinquent friends. A child will tend to look like the parent they most identify with. Notice how Jesus referred to Himself as looking at, or watching Me, and doing what I do. Notice how He repeatedly went alone to be with Me.

Jesus began the process of restoring you to My image by dying and giving His Blood, so you could be forgiven of your sins. That was only the beginning of the process. Sadly, many people stop right there at the beginning, so they never are transformed into My image. They are still marred - forgiven, yes, but marred. What makes a child become just like his parent or a person like their friend? Fellowship. Constant, intentional fellowship. Agreement. Identification. Desire to conform. I want you, Little Pearl, to remain in Our Presence, but not just as an observer. What will restore you back to My image is union with Us. The more you union with Us, the more you will be conformed into Our image. It is impossible to not reflect light and love when you have been infiltrated with it. This is why Paul said to be filled with all the fullness of God. How else are you to be conformed to My image?

Come to Us as a little child, ready to be molded. Spend time in Our Presence - Father, Son, and Holy Spirit - and union with Us. Let Us restore you to Our likeness.

HIS PEACE　　　　　　　　　　　3/20/13 a.m.

Little Pearl, My peace I give to you. Not as the world gives . . . the world seeks peace through many methods. These are not the way to receive peace. The way to receive peace is through complete submission to My Will. You are being flooded with peace, because you are releasing everything in your life, including your life, to Me. The more you are willing for Me to take away, if I choose, the more peace you have. The more you die to your desires, self, relationships, events, things - everything - the more peace you have. The more I Am your only desire, the more peace you have.

HIS PLEASURE   3/21/13

Oh, send out Your light and Your truth! Let them lead me; Let them bring me to Your holy hill and to Your tabernacle. Then I will go to the altar of God, to God my exceeding joy; and on the harp I will praise You, O God, my God.

Psalm 43:3-4

For the Lord takes pleasure in His people; He will beautify the humble with salvation.

Psalm 149:4

They are abundantly satisfied with the fullness of Your house, and You give them drink from the river of Your pleasures.

Psalm 36:8

You will show me the path of life; in Your presence is fullness of joy; at Your right hand are pleasures forevermore.

Psalm 16:11

As the bridegroom rejoices over the bride, so shall your God rejoice over you.

Isaiah 62:5b

Jesus -
Pearl, I take pleasure in you. I enjoy you. I know that is a new thought for you, but I have great pleasure from you. Your obedience brings Me pleasure. Submission and blind faith pleasure Me. You feel this pleasure in My Presence. I want you to know that I feel pleasure from you as well. This is a real relationship that We have. Relationships which are intimate, and based on true love

and sacrifice for each other, are enjoyable and are full of pleasure. Enjoy the pleasure. It is mutual.

Marriage was designed by Father to be pure pleasure. Unity brings pleasure. So few seek unity with Me, but those who do experience the pleasure of real Life. All others look for a substitute. Don't wonder about this pleasure - We know what true pleasure is - the love and unity in Our intimate relationship. That is the Holy of Holies, My Presence with you, enveloped by pure Love.
Come away with Me, My Pearl of Great Price. The more you give, the more you will receive. This principle is applied to your will and all areas of your life. The more you let go, accept My Will, My circumstances I placed you in, give control of them to Me, listen for My instruction, give your desires up to Me, then the more you will receive of My Presence. If you desire Me, then you must give all to Me. The more you give, the more you will receive.

The Lord gives, the Lord takes away, blessed be the name of the Lord. Though He slay me, yet will I trust Him. The more you give, the more you will receive. Will you trust Me and truly lay down your life for Me?

CHOICE WORDS ARE FEW　　　　　　　　3/23/13

My Precious Pearl, a wise man once said that an entire city could be won by very few words. Choice words, accompanied by a heart of love, have the blessing of the Holy Spirit. The few words that are spoken by a soul that is in complete submission to Me contain the force of a major earthquake. The soul that trusts in Me and is completely accepting of what I Am doing can speak from a position of freedom from selfish desires or agendas. Therefore, the choice words are few, wise, true, and motivated by love for Me.

Submission to My Will is the key. Surrender completely to My Hand. I can make a foolish rebellious heart turn on a dime. I can make a fool's decisions work for My own purposes. The only thing you have to do is let your words be very few, trust Me, and watch My Hand move. You will be thrilled, as I show-off for you.

You will see Me show-off for you as a guy who wants to court a girl. Sure, sunsets, beaches, mountain ranges and other things in nature are ways I show-off to you, but, Pearl, I can show-off in the relationship problems around you as well. I can display magnificence while beating up the spiritual bad guys, just like in the movies. Watch Me show-off for you. I love you.

TRUE SACRIFICE INVOLVES PAIN   3/24/13 a.m.

Holy Spirit -
My Pearl, You died for Jesus again. Unless two agree, how can they walk together? How can the darkness agree with the light? You cannot minister to those in darkness without pain. You will be wounded every time. Those who allow oppressive spirits to use them are themselves in pain and wound others. Sacrificing yourself, your spirit and body, in this way causes that deep pain. Continue to come to Me each time and I will heal you.

When I heal sacrificial wounds, they are not only healed, but your spirit is expanded to be stronger and able to receive more of Our Presence. The peace you now feel is in direct contrast to that pain. You can testify to others of the wounding from your voluntary death, and the healing I give. Your sacrifice was not only accepted, but was a wonderful aroma to Jesus.

Papa will give you many more opportunities to suffer and die for Jesus, your Husband. It will always be your choice to share in His sufferings. When you obey and die out of love for your Husband, there will be pain. Expect the pain - it is not suffering without pain. Expect many painful deaths. Each time you offer yourself, your rights, your sense of justice, your desires on the altar, you become the seed that dies, and then new life begins. When you die, Papa releases great power. This power works miracles in the lives of those around you. Hearts hardened by the deceitfulness of sin become softened. Blind eyes gradually begin to see. Those whose spirits are almost asleep - drugged by the lukewarm spirit of complacency - begin to wake up. This life-giving power is only released through sacrifice, like the sacrifice women make to birth their babies.

True sacrifice involves pain, or it is no sacrifice at all. But Pearl, with the death and subsequent life comes more intimacy with Jesus. You will feast at the table of His Presence. You will drink from the cup of His Love. You will have much in common, since you both share the experiences of death and suffering in obedience to Papa. You will intimately identify with each other, which will make your fellowship and marriage sweeter and sweeter.

As you continue on this marriage journey with Jesus, expect many opportunities to express your love for Him by dying for Him. Remember that, after Jesus received Me like a dove, I led Him into the wilderness to suffer. To suffer for another is to love. To love is to reflect the image of your Husband. The two go together. Remember though, that Jesus understands from personal experience what you are going through. Remember also that I will always be here to heal you and restore your spirit. Pearl, each time you volunteer to do the hard things, you become more and more beautiful to Jesus, your Lover.

(The following verses are from the Amplified Bible.)

I know whom I have chosen; but it is that the Scripture may be fulfilled, he who eats [his] bread with Me has raised up his heel against Me.

John 13:18b

Even My own familiar friend in whom I trusted (relied on and was confident), who ate of My bread, has lifted up his heel against Me.

Psalm 41:9

But Jesus replied, "You do not realize what you are asking. Are you able to drink the cup that I am about to drink and be baptized with the baptism with which I am baptized?" They answered, "We are able."
Matthew 20:22

Your eye is the lamp of your body; when your eye [your conscience] is sound and fulfilling its office, your whole body is full of light; but when it is not sound and is not fulfilling its office, your body is full of darkness.
Luke 11:34

But love your enemies, and be kind and do good-doing favors so that someone derives benefit from then; and lend expecting and hoping for nothing in return, but considering nothing as lost and despairing of no one; and then your recompense (your reward) will be great - rich, strong, intense and abundant - and you will be sons of the Most High; for He is kind and charitable and good to the ungrateful and the selfish and wicked. So be merciful - sympathetic, tender, responsive and compassionate - even as your Father is [all these]. Judge not - neither pronouncing judgment nor subjecting to censure - and you will not be judged; do not condemn and pronounce guilty, and you will not be condemned and pronounced guilty; acquit and forgive and release (give up resentment, let it drop), and you will be acquitted and forgiven and released. Give, that [gifts] will be given you, good measure, pressed down, shaken together and running over will they pour into [the pouch formed by] the bosom [of your robe and used as a bag]. For with the measure you deal out - that is, with the measure you use when you confer benefits on others - it will be measured back to you.
Luke 6:35-38

And Jesus called to [Him] the throng with His disciples, and said to them, If any one intends to come after Me, let him deny himself - forget, ignore, disown, lose sight of himself and his own interests - and take up his cross, and (joining Me as a disciple and siding with My party) follow with Me - continually, [that is] cleave steadfastly to Me. For whoever wants to save his [higher, spiritual, eternal] life, will lose [the lower, natural, temporal life which is lived (only) on earth], for My sake and the Gospel's will save [this higher, spiritual life in the eternal kingdom of God].

Mark 8:34-35

And He said, The kingdom of God is like a man who scatters seed upon the ground; Then continues sleeping and rising night and day while the seed sprouts and grows and increases, he knows not how. The earth produces [acting] by itself, first the blade, then the ear, then the full grain in the ear. But when the grain is ripe and permits, immediately he sends forth [the reapers] and puts in the sickle, because the harvest stands ready.

Mark 4:26-29

Always carrying about in the body the liability and exposure to the same putting to death that the Lord Jesus suffered, so that the [resurrection] life of Jesus also may be shown forth by and in our bodies. For we who live are constantly [experiencing] being handed over to death for Jesus' sake, that the [resurrection] life of Jesus also may be evidenced through our flesh which is liable to death. Thus death is actively at work in us, but [it is in order that our] life [may be actively at work] in you. Yet we have the same spirit of faith as he had who wrote, I have believed, and therefore have I spoken. We too believe, and therefore we speak. Assured that He Who raised up the Lord Jesus will raise us up also with Jesus and bring us [along] with you into His presence. For all [these] things are [taking place] for your sake so that the more the grace (divine favor and spiritual blessing) extends to more and more people and multiplies through the many, the more the thanksgiving may increase [and abound] to the glory of God.

II Cor. 4:10-15

Pearl -

After I was alone and in the Presence of the Lord, the Holy Spirit spoke to me and told me to go to sleep. I immediately fell into that unique sleep that is not normal - it is very different - I don't know how to describe it other than very sweet, and oh - goodness - light, tingles, floating, I really can't describe it. I continued to hear the Holy Spirit speaking while I was sleeping, but could not tell what was said.

When I awoke, I asked, "What did You say to me, and why could I not hear or understand clearly?" The Holy Spirit replied, "Because I was speaking to your spirit, not to your mind. You do not need Me to always speak to you with understanding. That is why some tongues are not to be interpreted. It is communication only between your spirit and Me."

When I woke, I could immediately tell that the pain, heaviness and oppressive feelings were gone. I really was healed. It was late, but I had energy and a light feeling. My joy and peace have been restored. The memory is faded - like nothing happened - only better. My time with Jesus was also super-sweet. So worth all the pain and sacrifice. I really recommend dying to your flesh - so hard, painful and horrible, but afterward the healing and sweetness of fellowship is amazing!

OVERWHELMED BY HIM 3/ 24/13

Pearl -

Jesus, You visited me in Your passionate, fierce Love night before last. You gave me a taste of Your almost aggressive, violent love for me. I came close to Your raw power, raw love, and heard You claim me as Your own in forceful, dangerous, passionate love. You claimed me as Your possession, Your territory, Your wife. It was a fierce declaration, like a lion who is claiming his portion and letting all the others in the pack know that, if they come near his portion, he will rip them apart.

Jesus, I am gone . . . sunk . . . a hot mess. I now cannot even function. When this encounter was over, all I could do is cry, mourn, and yearn for more of You. I thought I was in love with You before, but now I cannot even describe this obsession. Perhaps those on crack cocaine understand. Every cell in my body is screaming for You. I am more lovesick than Romeo and Juliet could ever hope for. The word, "desire," does not help at all. Last night Your Presence was here all night. Your wonderful massage was all over me, Your gentle ways, caresses ... but Jesus ... I am crying, hungering, craving more. I love these benefits of Your Presence. I am truly thankful. I love sensing You throughout the day, feeling You in public like a lover's secret ... but I want more. Now that I have tasted You - Jesus the God/Man - I am miserable. I am a wreck.

Your intense masculinity has every female cell in my body screaming and drooling. Your raw power scares me, but awakens desire in me for You at the same time. I will never watch a chic flick again. What a pitiful substitute all others are compared to You. Laughable. Boy, do Americans have the wrong picture of You!

Now I am the most miserable of all Your creatures. How can I go on like this? Jesus, I do love this wonderful Presence of Yours, but now that I have experienced You - Your Person - Your Manhood - nothing else will satisfy me. I love Your benefits, but what I really want is You. It's like being married to a very rich man. You love the houses, boats and vacations, but what you really want is the man himself. Jesus, I want You again. All that is on the earth - objects, relationships - all are nothing to me compared to my desire for another ten seconds with You.

Now I understand the huge sacrifice Paul made for the church. He said he longed to be with You, but was willing to make the huge sacrifice of not being with Your physical Presence, in order to help the struggling church get started. Now I understand what You, Jesus, really suffered while on the cross. The physical pain was terrible. The weight of all our sin was crushing, but the really excruciating pain came from being separated from the Father. I just had a taste of You, and I can't function. Please have mercy on me. All I can do is beg, cry, and hold on to hope that You will return.

I understand that I am to wait. You have told me to wait for many things - hard things - in the past. Having patience and endurance have never been easy for me. Well now, we are in a whole new ball game. To have to wait to have You with me like that is sheer torture. How can I go on? Think straight? Smile? Carry on conversation? Holy Spirit, only You can help me survive this wait. I am begging. What a pitiful, miserable mess I am now. Even so, I would not change a thing. Jesus, Your visit was the most wonderful thing that had ever happened to me. Even in this horrible pain of longing, I am so grateful and would have it no other way.

So . . . I wait . . . I pant like the deer pants for water during an August drought . . . I look for my next "fix" like a drug addict . . . I cry and hide the tears from everyone around me. Again, Jesus, I thank You for this sense of Your Presence, for Your still, small Voice in my spirit. But Jesus, to hear You speak aloud to me as You did night before last . . . to be with You . . . to experience You like that . . . I am gone, ruined for anything else. Keep the riches - just please give me the Man!!

By night on my bed I sought the one I love; I sought him, but I did not find him. "I will rise now," I said, "and go about the city; in the streets and in the squares I will seek the one I love." I sought him, but I did not find him. The watchmen who go about the city found me; I said, "Have you seen the one I love?" Scarcely had I passed by the, when I found the one I love. I held him and would not let him go, until I had brought him to the house of my mother, and into the chamber of her who conceived me.
Song of Solomon 3:1-4

I opened for my beloved, but my beloved had turned away and was gone. My heart leaped up when he spoke. I sought him, but I could not find him; I called him, but he gave me no answer. The watchmen who went about the city found me. They struck me, they wounded me; the keepers of the walls took my veil away from me. I charge you, O daughters of Jerusalem, if you find my beloved, that you tell him I am lovesick!
Song of Solomon 5:6-8

What is your beloved more than another beloved, O you fairest among women? What is your beloved more than another beloved, that you should give us such a charge? [She said:] My beloved is fair and ruddy, the chief among ten thousand. His head is precious as the most fine gold; his locks are curling and bushy, and black as a raven. His eyes are as doves beside the water brooks, bathed in milk and fitly set. His cheeks are as a bed of spices or balsam, as banks of sweet herbs yielding fragrance. His lips are like blood-red anemones or lilies, distilling liquid (sweet smelling) myrrh. His hands are as rods of gold, set with [nails of] beryl or topaz. His body is a figure of bright ivory overlaid with [veins of] sapphire. His legs are as strong and steady pillars of marble set upon bases of fine gold; his appearance is like Lebanon, excellent, stately and majestic as the cedars. His voice and speech are exceedingly sweet; yes, he is altogether lovely - the whole of him delights and is precious. This is my beloved, and this is my friend, O daughters of Jerusalem!

Song of Solomon 5:9-16 Amplified

PS: I can't stop listening to William McDowell's "Wrap Me in Your Arms." It is on repeat on my Ipod Nano and playing in my ears day and night.

LOVESICK FOR JESUS 3/24/13 p.m.

Pearl -

After Friday night's visitation from Jesus, I grieved and yearned all weekend. He has now healed me and given me peace. He had to keep reassuring me over and over. Now I have accepted the state of His Presence . . . more than before the visit, but not like the visit. He has replaced mourning with fulfillment, and longing with peace. I can now function and smile. I know that He will return like that, and have submitted my will to the current state of our togetherness.

Now I know what the word "overwhelmed" really means. Other words have changed for me as well . . . words like "hero" and "passion" and "intensity" and "power" and "love" and "fear" and "secure" and "desire." He has already told me that when I am in His Presence face to face, I will faint. I am sure I will faint repeatedly. I had to sleep on and off all weekend from the exhaustion of the encounter and my emotional response. Now I am restored.

Jesus -

Pearl, you are now seeing many of your sins which you were blind to before. You see your sinful flesh as it dictated your mothering of your children. You are seeing your sinful flesh as you are remembering clashes in your marriage. Seeing your past sin and foolishness is beneficial for increasing your wisdom and humility in the present. It is not beneficial for anything else. Therefore, draw wisdom and humility from the memories, but leave the past in My Hands. When the time is right, apologize for your sin and ask forgiveness. Then release all to Me. Do not worry about whether or not others see your new heart.

Let everything go and continue to live with Me. Remember that there is no one else allowed in Our relationship - just you and Me. The journey we are taking is Ours alone, so remain in the present with Me.

As you therefore have received Christ Jesus the Lord, so walk in Him, rooted and built up in Him and established in the faith, as you have been taught, abounding in it with thanksgiving.

Col. 2:6, 7

Not that I have already attained, or am already perfect; but I press on, that I may lay hold of that for which Christ Jesus has also laid hold of me. Brethren I do not count myself to have apprehended; but one thing I do, forgetting those things which are behind and reaching forward to those things which are ahead, I press toward the goal for the prize of the upward call of God in Christ Jesus.

Phil. 3:12-14

But the meek shall inherit the earth, and shall delight themselves in the abundance of peace.

Psalm 37:11

Book One

THE CIRCLE OF LOVE 3/25/13

Jesus, this feeling of being filled with the fullness of You is amazing. Hearing Your Voice and living in You have become my entire life. Now I know what the verse, "In You I live and move and have my being" means. How empty I was before and had no idea. How lonely I was before, but ignorant of the depths of my loneliness.

To say, "I love you," does not do justice to the expression of my love. Obedience does not fully express my love for You. Yet, I have a need deep inside me to express this amazing love that I have for You. I now know the only way to express that love to satisfaction is for all my other desires to die for You. Serving You, in dying for You, is the only way I can express my love for You adequately.

Jesus -

Pearl, We are in a circle of Love. We love together. We desire to serve each other and express Our Love. Therefore, we die for each other. I then resurrect you to newness of life in Me. You emerge healed and with a greater capacity for loving Me and containing My Presence. Then your desire to die for Me and to express your love for Me increases. We then take the plunge again. The circle of Love continues getting deeper, sweeter, richer, fuller, and more powerful. Our circle becomes a vortex that begins to suck others in. It's a powerful force. You are already seeing the lives of others around you change. That is the beginning. There is no greater force in the universe than the power of Love. Our Love, unleashed in this circle, will shake loose the shackles of hell. I Am so in love with you, Pearl. The passionate force you feel surging throughout your being is only a fraction of My Love. I have to hold back, or My Love for you will overwhelm you and cause you to faint. You now feel it, even when sleeping. I am like a bridegroom who cannot keep his hand off his new bride. I Am consumed with passion and desire for you. You are Mine. I own you. I have pleasure - great pleasure in you. Come away with Me, My Pearl.

CHIP AWAY
3-25-13 p.m.

Pearl -

Jesus, being corrected, ill-thought-of, and accused is an event that I accept from Your Hand. Humiliation is necessary to chip away pride. I want to be a beautiful bride for You. My pride is ugly. If these humbling circumstances will make me humble and more pliable in Your Hands, then I submit to them. I will not defend myself or fret over the injustice. I lay before You, and ask that You use what the enemy means for harm to create beauty in me. Do whatever it takes to make me beautiful to You. I desire nothing and no one else. Show me how to please You.

LET GO OF EVERYTHING　　　　3-26-13 a.m.

Jesus -
Pearl, abandon yourself to Me. Let go completely of everything in your body, your mind, your past, your future, your feelings - everything. Relax and trust Me. Abandonment of your self to Me is faith. You have asked Me how you can please Me as My wife. A gentle, quiet spirit of abandonment to Me is the way to My Heart - to please Me above all else. I melt.

Pearl -
Jesus, You gave me the most wonderful experience with You yesterday morning. Then, after several humbling experiences yesterday, I could not sense Your Presence as well. I admit that I began to fear losing You. You and Your Presence are more to me than anything, and I could not live without You. So Jesus, I did a terrible thing. I began to fear, doubt, and, if You had not intervened, I would have fallen into panic. How could I experience such awesome moments with You, hearing and feeling Your Love for me, but yet quickly let doubt and fear take over my mind when I don't sense You? I will never judge and look down in self-righteousness on the Israelites again for their unfaithfulness and doubt. We, in our arrogance during Bible studies, have marveled at the crossing of the Red Sea and other experiences of the Israelites, and then called them dumb for doubting Your ability to take care of them in the wilderness. I basically did the same thing. You have given me so many wonderful faith-building experiences, but yet, after humbling experiences, and then my time with You was not as full of Your Presence as before, what did I do? I crumbled into fear and doubt. I almost panicked. Oh Lord, I believe. Help thou my unbelief. What a pitiful

wife I am for You! I am so sorry for judging the Israelites. My pride obviously needed these lessons.

Jesus -
Pearl, the more you abandon yourself to Me, the easier it will be to trust Me when you don't sense Me. If I choose to work in a way that you cannot sense as well, then accept it, knowing that I Am still in control. I may be behind you, but I Am still there. Accept every event as coming from My loving Hand and a part of My loving plan. Accept even what may feel like My withdrawal. I have a purpose in everything. Sometimes My plan is a faith-building exercise for you. Sometimes it is a cutting away of your pride and tendency to judge. I never stop shaping you, and forming you to My image. I have many tools to do this - tools of love and passion, tools of the mistreatment of others, tools of diminishing your sensing of My Presence. Just know that I will never leave you or forsake you . . . no matter what you feel.

Pearl -
Jesus, that word "forsake" makes me remember Your words on the cross, "My God, My God, why have You forsaken Me" (Mark 15:34)? Why did You say that? Surely You knew that the Father would not let You down.

Jesus -
Pearl, remember that I not only died for you, but I actually became sin for you. I became pride, lust, envy, rebellion, and all the others. I allowed Satan to put all the sins on Me. Pearl, that included the sin of unbelief or doubt. I became unbelief and doubt, as well as the other sins. Yes, I knew the Father's plan ahead of time. I also knew that He could not be with Me for a time, since light and darkness cannot be together. Yes, I knew He

would not leave Me there and forsake Me forever - knew this before I took on the cross. But, as I took the sin of doubt upon Myself, I allowed you and all My followers to hear that I provided atonement for their unbelief, as well as their other sins. The sin of unbelief separates you from the Father's Voice. My power works through faith. I had to take on that sin, so you could be delivered from doubt. Only then could you trust Me to the point of complete abandonment of your self. Pearl, your faith in Me, in spite of My loving experiences, wavered and became doubt. I understand. I am a Savior and Husband who understands. That is why I took on doubt and now forgive you.

Pearl -
Jesus, I am so overwhelmed with gratitude and a renewed appreciation that I am nothing and can do nothing without you. I feel so stupid. I will never judge the Israelites again. Now when I see Your huge sacrifice for me, Your love, Your taking doubt and unbelief for me, which caused You unspeakable pain, as You were not only separated from the Father, but also without faith to know that it was only temporary - now my sacrifices and dying to self seem pitifully small. I can never look at my sacrifices and suffering the same again. They must look like a child's mud pie to You.

Jesus -
Pearl, every one of them is a treasure to Me. Whenever you die to your self, in faith and obedience to the point of pain, I Am enraptured with intense Love for you. My focus on you is like a powerful laser beam. My Love for you is like the explosion of a star - but with even greater force and power.

Pearl to Papa God -
Papa, I think I am the most needy of all your children. Thank You for giving Jesus to me. My heart is so full of need and gratitude at the same time, and just the fact that you are my Papa and all that means - I am overwhelmed.

PAPA SPEAKS ON WAITING-PSALM 62   3/26/13 p.m.

Papa -
Pearl, read Psalm 62. *Truly my soul silently waits for God; from Him comes my salvation. He only is my rock and my salvation; He is my defense; I shall not be greatly moved. How long will you attack a man? You shall be slain, all of you. Like a leaning wall and a tottering fence. They only consult to cast him down from his high position; they delight in lies; they bless with their mouth. But they curse inwardly.*

My soul, wait silently for God alone, for my expectation is from Him. He only is my rock and my salvation; He is my defense; I shall not be moved. In God is my salvation and my glory; the rock of my strength, and my refuge, is in God. In God is my salvation and my glory; The rock of my strength, and my refuge is in God. Trust in Him at all times, you people; pour out your heart before Him; God is a refuge for us. Surely men of low degree are a vapor, Men of high degree are a lie; If they are weighed on the scales, they are altogether lighter than vapor. Do not trust in oppression, nor vainly hope in robbery; If riches increase, do not set your heart on them. God has spoken once, twice I have heard this: That power belongs to God. Also to You, O Lord, belongs mercy; for You render to each one according to his work.

Follow My instructions in this Psalm. These instructions are for both when you are engaged during your busy day, as well as when you are alone with Me in My Presence. They are for times of stress and times of intimacy with Me. Hear these instructions:

1. Truly my soul silently waits for God.
2. My soul, wait silently for God alone.

3. Trust in Him at all times, you people; pour out your heart before Him.
4. Remember that power belongs to God.

Wait. Wait for Me all the time. Pearl, waiting for Me involves trust. Action on your part means you think you have to do something or it won't get done. Wait. When you seek My Presence, begin to wait. When circumstances are hard, begin to wait. Waiting also involves surrender. You are abandoning your will and receiving Mine. Surrender. Wait. Wait silently. Calm yourself like a child who was upset, but now is with his mother. Wait in reverent silence. You are in the Presence of the Most Holy God. Be silent in your humility, awe, and respect. When in the middle of hard circumstances, be silent. You cannot hear My Voice if you are venting your emotions. Be silent as you defer to My control of the situation. Silently wait for Me.

If you need to vent, come to Me and pour your heart out in private. Vent to Me. I love you and won't condemn. As you lay your heart out, the two of us will begin to dissect both the circumstances and your heart together. Remember that to hear My Voice, you must wait and be silent. Therefore, vent and then wait in silence. You will hear My Voice or become aware of the Truth concerning the circumstances and your own heart. I may reveal Truth over a period of time, so continue to wait. Be silent.

At all times and in all circumstances, remember that all power is Mine. I Am not small. Therefore, wait in awe, respect, and expectation. Be silent in trust, humility, and peace. Practice this, My Pearl. Abandon yourself to Me.

PAPA CONTINUES   3/28/13 a.m.

Papa continues:
Pearl, read Psalm 85:8, *"I will hear what God the Lord will speak, for He will speak peace to His people and to His saints. . ."* I Am the Lord your God, your Maker, your Husband. I Am highly motivated to speak to you. I Am more motivated to have a close relationship with you than you can imagine. No one ever needs to think that I Am far away and prefer silence. Listen to My Voice all day long. I speak peace. I speak to your spirit, not your mind.

Now turn to John 4:22-24. If you do not know Me, the truth about Who I Am, what I Am about, then how can you and I be intimate? I want intimacy with you. Therefore, I want you to experience Me and hear My Voice more and more. Then you will understand Worship, and a desire for intimacy will fill you when you know Me. *" . . . True worshipers will worship the Father in spirit and in truth; for the Father is seeking such to worship Him. God is Spirit, and those who worship Him must worship in spirit and truth."*

Pearl, keep talking to Me with your spirit. Keep listening to Me in your spirit. Continue living out of your spirit. Continue withdrawing from your mind. Do not trust your mind. It is carnal. The enemy can manipulate your mind. I Am Spirit. I speak to and live with your spirit. We have intimate fellowship because you are remaining in your spirit, in My Spirit. My Voice and Presence are continually renewing your spirit. It is truly a dry and thirsty land, where there is no water, for those whose spirits do not commune with My Spirit.

I will send some to you who have no idea how to receive the River of Living Water into their spirit. I Am their Good Shepherd. Therefore, it is My desire to refresh them with My Living Water. You and I will teach them where their river is located, and how to drink Life and Truth from it. Then they also will know Me for themselves and have intimacy with Me. Peaceful, joyful intimacy is what I want to have with My children.

Remember the pain you felt when you considered the possibility of your future grandchildren growing up in a distant, foreign country, speaking a foreign language, understanding only a foreign culture, and never knowing you, their grandmother who loves them? You envisioned them only knowing you as a face on a screen or words in emails. You felt pain, because you knew you would remain as a stranger to them, and not be a real part of their lives. That is how I feel about My people, Pearl, who do not know how to have real intimacy with Me. They do not hear My Voice or enter My Presence for themselves. They may occasionally read My "email" or hear someone talk about Me, but you and I both know that is not knowing Me and having intimacy with Me. It truly is a dry and thirsty land where there is no water. There are still sheep of Mine who desperately want to hear My Voice. Read Isaiah 41:17-18 *The poor and needy seek water, but there is none. Their tongues fail for thirst. I, the Lord, will hear them; I, the God of Israel, will not forsake them. I will open rivers in desolate heights, and fountains in the midst of the valleys; I will make the wilderness a pool of water, and the dry land springs of water.*

Now, Pearl, read John 4:14 . . . *but whoever drinks of the water I shall give him will never thirst. But the water that I shall give him will become in him a fountain of water springing up into everlasting life.*

Continue listening to My Voice, Pearl. Continue living with Me in your spirit. Our intimacy will grow throughout eternity. I Love you, My Pearl of Great Price.

HOLY SPIRIT TEACHES   3/28/13 p.m.

My sweet Pearl, I cannot help but smile each time you ask Me to teach you. How do you maintain a gentle and quiet spirit when you are in a conflict, being accused, yelled at, and otherwise involved in painful and disquieting circumstances? I know you have a heaviness in your spirit from your past failures. Give them to Me. Remember not to look backward at the past. You are forgiven, and everything will work for your good and the Father's glory.

As to your question pertaining to future difficult situations, spend more and more time with Me. That is all there is to it. Doing anything else will profit little. Using techniques for conflict resolution and anger management are man's way. If they did work, man would receive the glory. They may help some appear to be righteous on the outside, but they remain unchanged in their spirit. Just spend time with Me. As We fellowship together, I will smooth away wrong priorities, selfish desires, fears, and unbelief. People always take on the disposition and characteristics of those they have a close relationship with. Do not fret about your weaknesses and failures. Just spend each day with Me. I will create My fruit in you without any other effort from you. Many Bible studies and good works cannot do what I can do in a short time that is spent with one who is fellowshipping with Me. Just bring to Me your desire to learn and your focus on Us.

As We go through your days together, your spirit will absorb Me. At that point, out of the issues of your heart - Me - your mouth will speak. When you are tempted to be afraid or defensive, you will feel My gentle nudging, reminding you to be quiet and let Papa do His work in

the situation. As your spirit continues in the habit of remaining with Me, your mind won't spin out of control.
So, My sweet Pearl, let go of your mind. Live in your spirit with Me. I will do the rest. You may have some small failures to begin with, but We will make progress each day. Don't be discouraged. I Love you. I Am here to teach and help - not punish. I Am your Friend and Encourager. Relax and release your spirit into My Hands. Self-management techniques are shallow. No one can manage self anymore than he can tame the tongue. The flesh is full of sinful desires. Only I Am strong enough to overcome. Trust Me.

REMOVAL OF SOUL TIES 3/29/13 a.m.

Jesus -

Pearl, when I remove people from your life, it is because I want you all to Myself. Your soul is not to be tied to anyone else. You belong to Me exclusively. You are Mine and I Am yours. My primary interest is in Our relationship, yours and Mine. Therefore, I will use the others in your life to preserve the exclusiveness of Our relationship. Your relationships with certain ones are so difficult and even painful, because I want all of you to Myself.

Often those who have satisfying human relationships never seek Me or have any interest in Me beyond a shallow, cultural, obligatory service. Not you, Pearl. I want you. I want Us. Therefore, I will keep other hearts away. Yes, I will use you to minister to those around you. Yes, you will care for them, but not in a soul-tie.

Your soul is Mine. Your entire being is Mine. We are now married - you gave yourself to Me alone. So I tell you ahead of time, don't wonder at the people who were close to you beginning to back away. I will continue to bring others for Us, you and Me, to minister to, but those with whom you have had closeness will begin to fade away. You are complete in Me, and Me alone. I will fulfill you more and more. No one else is allowed in Our chamber. I Am your world. You are exclusively Mine. I will always take care of you and fulfill you. You don't ever have to be afraid again. I Am in your midst. You and I are joined together. I have taken possession of you.

"Sing and rejoice, O daughter of Zion! For behold, I am coming and I will dwell in your midst." says the Lord. "Many nations shall be joined to the Lord in that day,

and they shall become My people, and I will dwell in your midst. Then you will know that the Lord of hosts has sent Me to you." And the Lord will take possession of Judah as His inheritance in the Holy Land, and will again choose Jerusalem.

Zechariah 2:10-12

The great peace you feel coursing through your innermost being is the result of Our exclusive union. I Love you, Precious Pearl.

Pearl, I Love the way you continually come to My well of Love and drink deeply. You have learned that yesterday's water is not enough to sustain you today. Manna was always fresh. Remain abiding in the Vine. If you disconnect, the nourishment you received that day won't be enough for the next. We have had so many wonderful, intimate experiences together, but, as you have noticed, memories fade. You are continually bombarded with the darkness around you. Your spirit remembers Our intimate times, but your mind struggles with the details, because the forces of the world, demands of others, and your own flesh crowd the details and cause them to fade. Don't be alarmed or feel guilty. I know you treasure Our memories, justas I do. Just keep moving forward with Me. I will provide more and more intimate times together. We will face the giants around you together and win. We will have many date nights together. Papa, the Holy Spirit, and I will provide all the manna you need for each day.

You discovered a truth that those around you have yet to discover . . . My Living Water and My Presence are to be enjoyed continually. Church service, devotionals, Bible studies, and the occasional retreat are great, but they do not provide the continual flow of My Presence.

You have told others that you are addicted to My Presence. That is as it should be. You can do nothing without Me. Remain permanently connected to Me and I will flood your spirit with My Life. This is a great pleasure for Me.

BROKEN PIECES - MERCY TRIUMPHS   3/29/13 p.m.

Papa -

Little Pearl, you came to Me broken into small pieces. You were a ball of mangled spirit, wounded, torn apart, and pierced to the core. Your pain was so great that you begged me to end your life so very many times. I began to heal you with My Love and work a new meekness into your spirit. I healed your pain, but allowed your brokenness to develop into meekness. I restored joy, but allowed sorrow to develop into humility. As you began to release all your hopes, plans, and desires to Me, I breathed calmness into your spirit. With acceptance of My Will and complete surrender to Me came your ability to hear My Voice and sense My Presence. I then directed you to receive My deliverance and healing from many wounding events. With your newness of life came a new, intimate encounter with My Son, Jesus. I gladly gave Him to you, Little Pearl. He worked My Plan for you and redeemed your life that was destroyed.

Now that you and Jesus have this intimate relationship and life together as One, you continue to ask of Me the same request, over and over. Daily you ask Me for more of Jesus. More Voice. More Presence. More intimacy. More union. More of Jesus. Here is My reply, Little Pearl.

For to everyone who has, more will be given, and he will have abundance.   Matthew 25:29

Don't feel greedy or discontent with yourself. The more you have of Jesus, the more you want. You will be fulfilled, but yet continue to long for more at the same time. That is the effect He will always have on you. You will never stop longing for more of Him. You will never stop receiving more of Him. Your experiences with Him will grow richer, deeper, more meaningful, more amazing, more intimate, more loving, more healing, more tender, more powerful, more awesome. So My reply to your request is, "Yes." Yes, I will give you more of Jesus. Yes, I will give you more of the Holy Spirit. Yes, I will give you more of Myself. We know you have need of Us. Now you know how much you desire and crave Us. Now We will fulfill you each day, as your longing for Us grows each day. Your life with Us and Our Union together will only grow deeper, richer, and more intimate. You will never find the bottom of intimacy with Us. There is no bottom, Pearl. There is only abundance, and then more abundance. You are My little girl, My little Pearl.

How lovely is Your tabernacle, O Lord of hosts! My soul longs, yes, even faints for the courts of the Lord; My heart and my flesh cry out for the living God.
Psalm 84:1- 2

O God, You are my God; Early will I seek You; My soul thirsts for You; My flesh longs for You in a dry and thirsty land where there is no water.
Psalm 63:1

Who satisfied your mouth with good things; So that your youth is renewed like the eagle's.
Psalm 103:5

Holy Spirit -
My Sweet Pearl, you have been living what We call the abundant life. You are overflowing with the abundance of Our Presence and Love. With Our Presence comes not only great Love, but also understanding and wisdom. Peace remains within you rather than fear. You faith has

soared, so that you are not as disturbed by circumstances as before. You also have tasted the pleasures that come with Our Presence, and know what it is to be fulfilled, and even in ecstasy. Your only desire now is for more of Jesus and Our Presence. Sin is no longer enticing to you. The more you love Jesus, the more you crucify your sinful nature. Now the mere thought of displeasing Him makes you cry. This is the abundant life.

Remember to add one more element to your fellowship with Us, as you interact with those around you - abundance of mercy. Spending time in Our Presence has changed your soul. It has become like the new white, shiny, patent-leather shoes and white ankle socks trimmed with lace that your mother used to buy for you each Easter, when you were a little girl. You loved their white shininess. But when you wore them a few times, the scuffs from knocking them against surfaces appeared. Black scuff marks really stand out against the white, shiny patent-leather. You know to run to Jesus to clean your soul immediately. The problem is, My sweet Pearl, others don't. They do not live this abundant life in Our Presence. Now you not only see any little mark on your soul, you see the marks on theirs. Don't look down on them, as if you earned Our Presence. Remember that your intimacy with Us was an invitation. You accepted Our invitation, that is all. Therefore, when you see the fear, pride and selfishness in others' words and choices, consider them as people who have not begun an intimate journey with Us. Remember your own misery before Our intimacy, and have compassion. Mercy is always to triumph over judgment. I understand your feelings of distaste and sometimes you are repulsed. Allow your distaste to be covered by mercy.

When you changed your babies' soiled diapers, it was a distasteful job, but you still loved them. You were overjoyed with being a mother to them, despite the smelly mess. Be patient with the smelly mess around you now. Clean it as best as you can, with Me directing you. Gentle words turn away wrath. With quietness and gentleness, you and I can soften the hardest of hearts. Love covers a multitude of sins. Forgive and keep on forgiving. Those shiny, white, patent-leather shoes and ankle socks trimmed with lace will be noticed by those around you, when they reap the benefits from your Love. Ask Me for help. I Love helping you, My sweet Pearl.

Pearl -
When I was faced with a situation that was not going to change, I began to seek the Presence and Voice of the Lord more than I had ever before. I ran to the shelter of the shadow of His wings for protection. What I found there was startling. There was so much more than just protection under His wings. It is like running into a cave to find shelter from a surprise rainstorm, turning around, and then seeing Aladdin's storehouse of treasure. Under the Lord's wings, in His Secret Place, I found intense Love. That Love began healing my wounds, calming my fears, and changing my perspective. I found nourishment, as He Himself began to teach me. I fell madly in Love, as Jesus revealed Himself and His heroic, masculine, but tender qualities.

Yes, I was protected from the happenings in my life, but there was so much more. Now I don't care if the losses are ever restored. There is already some vindication, but it does not matter to me. I am no longer interested in restoring what I lost. My former life as a Christian was great, but I am happy to let it go in exchange for the treasure I now have in Jesus. There really is no comparison. The shadow of His wings is full of intimacy, intense love, peace, wisdom, joy, and pleasure. I know why . . . it is because Jesus, the Father, and the Holy Spirit are there waiting to fellowship and love on me. What can compare to that?

BATTLE IN THE MIND   3/31/13

Papa -
Little Pearl, most of your difficult battles take place in your mind. If one of Satan's fiery darts can successfully lodge itself in your mind, then the fire from it quickly spreads, until discouragement and pain set in. The one thought, negative interpretation of circumstances, prediction of the future, or bad memory, can become wedged into a weak area of your mind. From there, it spreads like a fire feeding on human logic, more bad memories, more tragic future possibilities, a sense of injustice or loss, until your whole mind is consumed under the pressure of the heat. You saw how quickly the heaviness of doubt and discouragement can descend upon your spirit from a burning mind. Don't be disappointed or condemn yourself when you cannot feel My Presence during those attacks. At this point, you cannot hear from your spirit. The smoke from your flaming mind obscures everything. Know that I Am still just as present with you, as I was during our most intense times together.

When the fire started in your mind, your consciousness rushed to it to deal with the flames. As you soon discovered, you have nothing in your own consciousness or inner being to put out the flaming thoughts. The enemy is particularly cruel when he adds more outside circumstances to fuel your already flaming brain. Now he has accomplished two goals - inflaming your mind with tormenting thoughts to focus your attention there, and veiling My Presence and Voice within your spirit with the smoke. Pearl, when this happens, know that you are under spiritual attack. Remember who you are - My precious Pearl. Remember Who I Am - Your Lord, Father, and Husband Who loves you with all passion.

Remember that I Am - Most High God with all power. Remember Our covenants We made together - the covenant of forgiveness, the covenant of marriage. Rehearse My promises that are written for this purpose. Choose two to meditate upon. Remember the authority that I gave to you when I gave you My Name - use it. Remember to get away from everyone and pour your mind out to Me. I Am the only One Who can extinguish the flames and clear the smoke. Peace will then return.

When you did this today, I then put you to sleep. You felt My Presence in and around you in your sleep. My Love was healing you and restoring your peace. When you woke, you immediately knew you were restored. Your mind was healed and your consciousness was back in your spirit with Me. I will always heal you, Little Pearl. Learn to repel those thoughts by recognizing where they came from. This will become like the physical body's immune system. Your spirit will become more efficient at recognizing the attacks from the onset. You will then repel the thoughts before they can become lodged in your mind. Your consciousness will remain with Me in your spirit and your mind will no longer have a voice. After such a battle, Little Pearl, come and spend the rest of the evening deep in your spirit - in My temple, under the shadow of My wings - with Me. Remember Our past intimate times. Focus on My Love. Remain with My Presence in your spirit. I will fill you with joy as you worship in your love for Me. I will never leave you or forsake you, Little Pearl. Your face is always in front of Me. I Am holding you in the palm of My Hand. You will not fall. Your future is dictated by My Love for you, not by those around you. No one can reach you in Our Secret Place. Follow My instructions. Love your enemies. Pray for them and show them mercy.

I AM GOD   3/31/13 p.m.

Papa – (with a powerful voice)
Little Pearl, I AM GOD to YOU! Remember when you were going through great tragedy and crying out to Me in desperation, "Oh God, be God to me!" At that time you had certain expectations of Me. Little Pearl, your expectations were too small. You only expected Me to restore. Now I want you to hear Me. I AM GOD to YOU! I AM YOUR GOD. I AM GOD.

Think about what that means. I AM all power, all force, all light, all energy, all passion, all Love. I AM fiercely GOD TO YOU. Fiercely. I fiercely protect you. I powerfully surround you. I forcefully deliver you. I powerfully hold you to Myself. I AM passionately jealous over you. I unleash unlimited energy against all who would come against you. Only My plan for you will prevail. I AM GOD to YOU! I WILL ALWAYS BE GOD TO YOU! THE ONE AND ONLY GOD.

I AM FOCUSED ON YOU, PEARL. Feel My raw power, energy, and passion for you. All other forces on earth are laughable. You never have to worry or be afraid again. You will have trials and forces that oppose you, but not for long. Little Pearl, I AM GOD TO YOU! I will crush all forces that come against My Pearl of Great Price. I will always deliver you. I may allow you to wait for My Plan to play out, but understand, Pearl, I AM GOD TO YOU. I AM YOUR GOD . . . YOUR GOD . . . YOUR GOD . . . YOUR GOD. I will roar with the force of all the oceans put together on your behalf. Nothing can stand against Me. I AM YOUR GOD. You belong to Me exclusively. I AM GOD to you, Little Pearl. Close your eyes, relax, sink into Me, and let Me show you what that means. You will sense the fierceness of My Powerful Passion for you. I AM GOD TO YOU.

PRISONER OF THE LORD 4/1/13 p.m.

Pearl, read Ephesians 4:1-2. Notice Paul's circumstances and his way of identifying himself. He truly was in prison, but he identified himself as being My prisoner.

I, therefore, the prisoner of the Lord, beseech you to walk worthy of the calling with which you were called with all lowliness and gentleness, with longsuffering, bearing with one another in love.

Now read Exodus 21:5-6.
"But if the servant plainly says, 'I love my master; my wife; and my children; I will not go out free.' Then his master shall bring him to the judges. He shall also bring him to the door, or to the doorpost, and his master shall pierce his ear with a awl; and he shall serve him forever."

Paul's relationship with Me was so deep, rich, intimate, and fulfilling that his highest pleasure was to be My prisoner, doing whatever I asked, remaining in the most painful of circumstances. He submitted his will, body, and spirit to My possession. When I led him to painful places with no end in sight, he simply, with a willing heart, took on the identity of one who is under the control of another to the point of torture.

In Exodus, if a slave loved his master excessively, to the point of preferring slavery to freedom, he allowed his body to be marked as one who is permanently owned by another by choice. He agreed to submit his will, body, and future to his master. Notice the absence of fear. Paul was not afraid to trust Me with total control. When I led him through horrible circumstances, he continued to claim he was My prisoner. He never asked to have his own will and freedom back. Not once did he change his mind. This is complete surrender.

You are also in difficult, sometimes excruciating circumstances. You could have changed your mind and removed yourself from the painful situation. Each day that you remained under My direction in those circumstances, you were My prisoner. Volunteer slaves and prisoners are those I can use best. I understand that the most difficult part is the future. A person could not know how long the painful condition will remain. Choosing to remain in My Will without hope that things will improve is a powerful sacrifice, one that is pleasing to Me, as it involves carrying the cross I have given you and being conformed to My image through the pain.

If I were to tell you that these circumstances will continue for another 10, 20, or 30 years, would you still submit to My Will? Would you continue to be My prisoner and slave? Every day that you ignore your desire for relief and submit to the situation I placed you in, you place a sweet-smelling sacrifice on the altar. It is a most holy and acceptable sacrifice. Paul knew the secret to reducing the pain of his prison. He embraced it. He did not hate, fight against, or resent his chains. Rather, he identified himself as one who wore My chains. The slave by choice identified himself with a voluntary mark on his body, so all the community would know that he was in a lowly, humiliating role by choice. Pearl, this is the highest form of faith and faithfulness. I do not take it lightly. I notice every submission of your will to Mine. When you accept the hard things as coming from My Hand and submit yourself to them, you are My prisoner and My slave. You take on the identity of one who has completely surrendered to Me. The fact that you do not know how long the situation may last makes your surrender to Me complete. You no longer seek to escape or change your situation. Now, even though there are times of real pain, you also have peace and even joy. You have My Presence with you. In effect, you surrendered freedom and ease for My Presence during captivity. This is the spirit of the martyrs - no self-pity, just abandonment to My Will.

When you are feel oppression, take on your identity as My voluntary prisoner and slave. Quietly submit. Love, serve, and give to those around you, without trying to defend yourself or demand change. Love your enemies or those who have put themselves in the position of enmity with you. Serve, give, and Love, while in your prison. You remain there by submission and choice and, therefore, there will be no self-pity. Submission to My Will and accepting the circumstances release high expectations that the kingdom of God will be advanced, whether you see the process or not.

Pearl, will you be My prisoner and My slave to the point of long-term suffering? Will you accept My offer blindly? I will continue to fill you, give you peace, and heal you. Our Love will only grow sweeter, richer, and stronger. Paul learned mysteries and experienced the richness of My Presence, while in great pain and humiliating circumstances. He knew the secret of embracing the circumstances to the point of identifying himself as My prisoner.

You and I would not have Our rich and meaningful times together, if you had not submitted and endured for years. The circumstances have not changed much, but look at the two of Us. We are on a continual honeymoon. I love you, Pearl, My slave and prisoner. One day you will know the effects of your voluntary imprisonment on the kingdom of God. Until then, be comforted with My Presence. Your prison and place of pain has become your ministry. Your slavery has become your volunteer work. Self-pity flees and joy returns!

THE TONGUE 4/2/13 p.m.

Little Pearl, read James 3:4-6:
"Look also at ships: although they are so large and are driven by fierce winds, they are turned by a very small rudder wherever the pilot desires. Even so the tongue is a little member and boasts great things. See how great a forest a little fire kindles! And the tongue is a fire, a world of iniquity. The tongue is so set among our members that it defiles the whole body, and sets on fire the course of nature; and it is set on fire by hell;" and James 4:6-11*:" But he gives more grace. Therefore He says: "God resists the proud, but gives grace to the humble." Therefore submit to God. Resist the devil and he will flee from you. Draw near to God and He will draw near to you. Cleanse your hands, you sinners; and purify your hearts, you double-minded. Lament and mourn and weep! Let your laughter be turned to mourning and your joy to gloom. Humble yourselves in the sight of the Lord, and He will lift you up. Do not speak evil of one another, brethren. He who speaks evil of a brother and judges his brother, speaks evil of the law and judges the law. But if you judge the law, you are not a doer of the law but a judge."*

Pearl -
Father, as I look back over my life, my heart is cut to the core when I remember the times I "vented" my feelings to someone. Then there are the times when I let my impatience become anger, and my anger turned into punishing words toward the very ones You gave me and I love so much! James is right when he describes the tongue as being like an out-of-control fire. I know there were times when stopping the words from coming out of my mouth would have been like stopping a freight train. I don't deserve Your Presence. You are so clean and I

have a dirtied mouth. Forgive me and cleanse me with Jesus' Blood. I want to remain in Your Presence. How painful it must have been for You to witness the way I allowed Satan to use my tongue to make me dirty and injure someone else.

Papa -
Little Pearl, when you come to Me confessing your sin, I cleanse you from all unrighteousness. From time to time, while We are fellowshipping together, I will do some Spring cleaning in your soul. Talking about your own sin is just half of what I want to discuss with you today. I also want you to see how vulnerable those around you are to their flesh and the enemy. You remembered how easy it was to sin with your tongue in the past. Once your tongue got started, it was nearly impossible to stop. Now think of those around you and their matching weakness. Yes, they have said terrible things to you and about you to others. Yes, poison continues to pour out of some. Just remember, Little Pearl, that they cannot stop the freight train any more than you could. Remember also that whomever you forgive, I forgive. Always look at the sin of others with a humble attitude and have compassion on them - even if the one they are accusing, attacking, or backbiting is you. Hell won't stop setting tongues on fire, but neither will I stop offering forgiveness.

Continue in the habit of asking the Holy Spirit's help in pressured situations. Continue spending your days in My Presence. You have already sensed the changes I have made in you. My Spirit not only shields you from the fiery darts of the enemy when spoken, but also prevents you from reacting in self-interest. With your self-interest gone, you no longer have any desire to vent, accuse, or become angry. The more you surrender to Me in My

Presence, the less you want for yourself in the world. The less you want, the less you fight to receive.

Continue to throw away your rights, Little Pearl. The world says you have rights to dignity, possessions, the kind of life you desire to live. Throw away those rights and, as you do, you will be less vulnerable to sin. Do not listen to the talk about your rights to boundaries. I will expose the enemy and protect you, as you make yourself subject or submissive to Me. I always take care of My Own. Wait in silence when others are using their tongues to hurt you. Jesus was silent in front of His accusers. Follow His example. He was silent when they spit on Him. He didn't vent or try to expose the injustice. He waited for Me. Re-read James 4:6. I promise to help you remain silent. You have already learned to limit your words. Continue to limit them. As your mom used to say, "Keep your thoughts to yourself." I make one change to that saying, "Continually take your thoughts to Me and Me alone." You and I will talk about everything all day long. This is the secret to preventing hell from setting your tongue on fire. Let's continue Our conversations. I love them. You love them. The enemy is stopped, and others notice the difference in the way you handle life. I Am glorified, and they become open to My work in them. Instead of a circle of pain, we now have a circle of Life. What's not to love? Let's talk, Little Pearl.

KINDNESS 4/3/13 a.m.

Papa -
Pearl, read Matthew 4:23-25:
And Jesus went about all Galilee, teaching in their synagogues, preaching the gospel of the kingdom, and healing all kinds of sickness and all kinds of disease among the people. Then His fame went throughout all Syria; and they brought to Him all sick people who were afflicted with various diseases and torments, and those who were demon-possessed, epileptics, and paralytics; and He healed them. Great multitudes followed Him - from Galilee, and from Decapolis, Jerusalem, Judea, and beyond the Jordan.

Pearl -
I was immediately aware of Jesus' intense kindness. How kind He was to let everyone know the truth about the Father's Love for them. How kind He was to spend all His time patiently healing each person of disease. I see His heart of compassion breaking for their ignorance of the Love that wants to hold them. I see His heart understanding their loneliness, fear, and confusion. I see Him feeling the worry of the parents for their sick babies. I see Him hurting with those who are in physical pain and fearing the dark future. I see Jesus rejoicing, as the needs of each person are met. He is happier for them than they are for themselves. I can't help but cry with the realization of Jesus' overwhelming love and absolute kindness. I have never met anyone as kind and loving as He is. I feel His kindness in every part of my being. He is kind to me over and over again. There is no limit to Jesus' kindness.

This makes me think of the areas in the United States where there are very few people who actually know and experience Jesus. I am aware of the lack of kindness in their community. Having tasted the kindness of Jesus myself, I now realize there is a built-in need, within my own soul, to experience kindness from another being. Jesus is allowing me to drink from His kindness and it is meeting those deep needs I never knew I had. Becoming aware of my need for His kindness brings me one step farther away from an attitude of self-sufficiency. I am becoming more needy every day - and loving it.

"... and He healed them." Some of the kindest words I have every read. I am so happy to be Jesus' Pearl! How proud I am of my Husband! How in love!

THE LION'S DEN   4/3/13 p.m.

Papa -

My Pearl, you have been in and out of the lion's den over and over for many years now. You know all about the lion's intimidating roar. You know the unpredictability of their attacks. You know their cruelty and illogic. They have allowed themselves to be used and manipulated by the enemy. My Pearl, I Am Mercy. Mercy, by its very nature, ministers to cruel lions. Mercy is received not for the loving, but for the weak, selfish, and hard-hearted lions. Mercy is not for the pure in spirit. It is reserved for those with contaminated hearts and twisted minds. Mercy is not extended to the kind and trustworthy, but to the cruel and hypocritical, whose blindness leads them to believe they are righteous and loving. Mercy is not for the thoughtful who demonstrate My Love, but for the self-centered judges who accuse and condemn in their blindness. I have called you to a daily attitude and service of mercy, My Pearl. Each time you are trapped in the lion's den, you are to put on My Mercy.

While in the lion's den, focus on Me, and I will place mercy in your spirit. My Mercy will replace the pain and humiliation you endure. Mercy will transform the circumstances from unbearable to ministry. Mercy will take you from being a victim to being one who heals and restores. Mercy will help you see the lion's own torment, rather than see the lion as your terminator.

After the time in the lion's den, come away to Me and pour out your pain. I will heal you. Your healed wounds will become points of strength in you. The humiliation you endured in silence will become honor. Remember that I Am always working. I work on the lions. You may not be able to see what I Am doing, but be confident that I Am working.

I Love you, My Pearl. Now come with Me, close your eyes, and enter the Secret Place. I will comfort you, give you peace, and heal you. Behold, I make all things brand new.

O Lord my God, I cried out to You and You healed me.
Psalm 30:2.

I WANT YOU TO LIVE 4/4/13

Little Pearl, you asked the question, "Why am I alive?" You asked out of intense pain and despair. It was a cry for mercy. My answer was, "Because I want you to live." Remember how I led you to meditate on the word, "live?" Not just exist. Not just be alive. Live. That means thrive and prosper. From that point, I took you through the valley of the shadow of death. We walked the whole valley together. Little Pearl, that walk was full of pain and suffering, but while you submitted and endured the process, not knowing if it would ever end, I was teaching and sculpting you. Because of that long walk, you now have the ability to hear My Voice and sense My Presence.

Now you know each day how much pleasure I have from you living. Your living in My Presence gives Me unspeakable joy. You now tell Me that you are the most blessed woman on Earth. Your pleasure and joy in My Presence are nothing compared to My delight in your presence. Yes, sweet Little Pearl, your presence is My delight. I crave you and your presence. I created you for My pleasure and I do take pleasure in you.

You are worthy, O Lord, To receive glory and honor and power; For You created all things, And by Your will they exist and were created.
Revelation 4:11

I know all your spots and wrinkles, but I still take pleasure in you. Now Our days together are spent in enjoying each other's presence. Even though most of your difficulties remain unchanged, the Valley of the Shadow of Death has become a Valley of Pleasures forevermore, Valley of Abundance of Joy, Valley of

Peace and Rest, Valley of Delightful Discovery. Our union with the Holy Spirit is intoxicating, full of pleasure and peace.

No, Little Pearl, you are not the only one who feels that delight during Our alone-times. I Am intoxicated with Our Union and Love-Jesus, Holy Spirit, you, and Me-a union, a reunion, a circle of fellowship, a firestorm of Love, a gentle peace, as gentle as the wind from a butterfly's wings, intoxicating, joyous. This experience is what Paul referred to as intoxication.

And do not be drunk with wine, in which is dissipation; but be filled with the Spirit.

Ephesians. 5:18

Continue to relax and enjoy Our Love. When you see others reacting to all manner of stresses - big and small - with fear, control, anger, and restlessness, then understand that they have not known My Love for them. Now you understand one of My tools for shaping you. You were sculpted with sharp, painful instruments in the Valley of the Shadow of Death. Now you are sculpted by My brush of Love and pleasure. Both instruments are necessary for real beauty and art. Hard hearts must be broken with sharp pain. Gentle and quiet spirits can then grow in peace and joy through the brushes of intoxicating Love and the pleasure of My Presence. I never wanted you to simply "exist." I want you to "live." I want you to thrive, grow, and prosper together with Me. You give me unspeakable pleasure. That is the answer to your pain-filled question.

For this reason I bow my knees to the Father of our Lord Jesus Christ, from whom the whole family in heaven and earth is named, that He would grant you, according to the riches of His glory, to be strengthened with might through His Spirit in the inner man, that Christ may dwell in your hearts through faith; that you, being rooted and grounded in love, may be able to comprehend with all the saints what is the width and length and depth and height - to know the love of Christ which passes knowledge; that you may be filled with all the fullness of God. Now to Him who is able to do exceedingly abundantly above all that we ask or think, according to the power that works in us, to Him be glory in the church by Christ Jesus to all generations, forever and ever. Amen. Ephesians 3:14-21

And we have known and believed the love that God has for us. God is love, and he who abides in love abides in God, and God in him. I John 4:16

And we know that the Son of God has come and has given us an understanding, that we may know Him who is true; and we are in Him who is true, in His Son Jesus Christ. This is the true God and eternal life.

I John 5:20

Yea, though I walk through the valley of the shadow of death, I will fear no evil; For You are with me; Your rod and Your staff, they comfort me. Psalm 23:4

How precious is Your loving kindness, O God! Therefore the children of men put their trust under the shadow of Your wings. They are abundantly satisfied with the fullness of Your house, and You give them drink from the river of Your pleasures. Psalm 36:7-8

For His anger is but for a moment, His favor is for life; Weeping may endure for a night, but joy comes in the morning. Psalm 30:5

I would have lost heart, unless I had believed that I would see the goodness of the Lord in the land of the living. Wait on the Lord; be of good courage, and He shall strengthen your heart; Wait, I say, on the Lord!
Psalm 27:13-14

You have turned for me my mourning into dancing; You have put off my sackcloth and clothed me with gladness.
Psalm 30:11

My Pearl, the way to hear My Voice and sense My Presence all day is to withdraw from your mind. Do not let your thoughts wander while in the shower, driving the car, or doing chores. Focus on your life with Me in your spirit. Each time you find yourself back in your mind, return it to Me in your spirit. This is a choice you make ... and act of your will ... a discipline of yourself. Never will you return to your spirit and find it empty. I will always be there. Walk in the Spirit-in your spirit. This is how you "sow to the spirit." By remaining with Me in your spirit, you will hear My Voice-My Living Word-and then your mind will be renewed as well. A mind that roams is a mind that is vulnerable. Wisdom and Truth will not come from your mind. My home is your spirit, so remain there with Me.

MY PRECIOUS PEARL   4/5/13

Jesus -
Pearl, read Romans 8:27 *Now He who searches the hearts knows what the mind of the Spirit is, because He makes intercession for the saints, according to the will of God.* Precious Pearl, I want you to understand the depth of My Love for you. I talk to Father about you all the time.

Pearl -
What do You say?

Jesus -
We talk about many things, but most often I thank Him for you. I Am amazed at His great gift of Love He gave to Me when He gave Me you. You see, Pearl, Father created you for Me. He knew how to form you - your spirit - in such a way that would delight Me. Remember that you are My reward. Father made you for Me, so I thank Him for His precious gift. I Am full of gratitude for you. He shares My joy in you. He shares My pleasure from you. My heart overflows with thanksgiving to Father for creating you, your spirit, and your personality, as a gift to Me. The Love He expressed, in giving you to Me as a gift, is amazing. You are My Precious Pearl. My bride. My gift from Father. I talk about you with thankfulness.

Pearl -
I am speechless.

CALLED TO BE A PEACEMAKER 4/5/13 p.m.

Jesus -
My Pearl, I have called you to be a peacemaker. Remember that peacemakers are not referees. A referee manages conflicts between others. A peacemaker is called to bring peace to conflicts in which they themselves are the target. How do you bring peace to the one who is hostile, angry, accusing, vengeful toward you? Mercy. You must be full of mercy. Peacemakers cannot make peace when they are preoccupied with defending themselves. When falsely accused by one who sees through the glass that is covered with unforgiveness and pride, you must be willing to see past injustice and into the lostness of his soul. You must remember that Truth is not seen by the blind. Justice is not found in those who do not know My Love. Mercy, Pearl.

Do not allow your mind to be caught up in the details of what the strife-filled person is saying, except to note any way in which you can apologize and receive correction. Withdraw from the rest of the words in your mind and remain with Me in your spirit. Then, once you have stabilized your inner self by connecting with Me, look for points of mercy.

Points of mercy are ways to empathize and show concern for the angry person. Points of mercy are ways that you can agree with some parts of his desires or argument. Points of mercy are given, even if the accuser is yelling, blindly speaking falsely, or out of control. Points of mercy are kind words that are spoken in gentleness. Points of mercy often look like unreasonable sacrifices, rather than compromise.

Be willing to go beyond what is fair and reasonable. Remember that blind people do not see reason. Use the power of Love. Humble yourself and say things like, "If I came across as that way to you, then I can see how you might feel frustrated." "If this is the way you see things, then I understand how you might feel_____." Do not be tempted to talk about your feelings in the heat of the moment. Rather talk about the angry one's interests, and how you can see his perceptions and the way they perhaps make him feel. Do not judge his selfishness or bitterness or fearful pride. Just find points of mercy. Leave lesson-teaching to Me. Leave your defense to Me. Leave the ultimate, long- term result to Me.

Sometime after the conflict, return to that one and offer anything you can to apologize and new understanding of something about his views. Give hugs of mercy and peace offerings of service. Peacemakers are not those who stand at the edge of the battlefield while others fight. A peacemaker is in the middle of the battle and usually is the one being attacked. Therefore, My Pearl, you will always come away with at least one wound.

Bring Me your soul-wounds as soon as you can be alone with Me, and I will heal them. I will restore your ability to forgive and re-arm you with the weapon of Love. Remember to avoid the mind-tugs of swirling thoughts in your head. Forget the details and do not analyze anything. Stay in your spirit with Me . . . not your mind. I will heal you in Our Secret Place.

My Pearl, don't be discouraged if you fail. Just continue learning. I will help you as you remain calm in the moment. When you fail, acknowledge your failure and apologize for all you can. You will make progress.

Remember that you will never be a peacemaker alone. I will always be there with you.

Bless those who curse you, and pray for those who spitefully use you. To him who strikes you on the one cheek, offer the other also. And from him who takes away your cloak, do not withhold your tunic either. Give to everyone who asks of you. And from him who takes away your goods do not ask them back. And just as you want men to do to you, you also do to them likewise.

But if you love those who love you, what credit is that to you? For even sinners love those who love them. And if you do good to those who do good to you, what credit is that to you? For even sinners do the same. And if you lend to those from whom you hope to receive back, what credit is that to you? For even sinners lend to sinners to receive as much back. But love your enemies, do good, and lend, hoping for nothing in return; and your reward will be great, and you will be sons of the Most High. For He is kind to the unthankful and evil. Therefore be merciful, just as your Father also is merciful.

Judge not, and you shall not be judged. Condemn not, and you shall not be condemned. Forgive, and you will be forgiven. Give, and it will be given to you: good measure, pressed down, shaken together, and running over will be put into your bosom. For with the same measure that you use, it will be measured back to you.

And He spoke a parable to them: Can the blind lead the blind? Will they not both fall into the ditch? A disciple is not above his teacher, but everyone who is perfectly trained will be like his teacher. And why do you look at the speck in your brother's eye, but do not perceive the plank in your own eye? Or how can you say to your

brother, 'Brother, let me remove the speck that is in your eye,' when you yourself do not see the plank that is in your own eye? Hypocrite! First remove the plank from your own eye, and then you will see clearly to remove the speck that is in your brother's eye.
Luke 6:28-42 (Amplified)

GOD ALWAYS WINS 4/7/13 p.m.

Pearl -

Papa, I am overwhelmed with a greater awareness of the fact that You win. You are the Winner. You win every time and You are not even challenged. You squash every opponent. They may be allowed to make noise and even "mouth-off" at You, but not for long. You had me read Isaiah 40-45 and the fact that You win is everywhere. We will see You destroy all who oppose You.

Papa, I am so proud to have You as my Papa. I am proud to be Your daughter. I am proud to say, "Look at Him! He's my Papa! Look at what He did!" No one can stop You, Papa. Your Great Plan worked. You are brilliant, and Your infinite strength makes Your enemies and all our troubles seem very small. Your plan was executed by Jesus and it worked. I am so proud that You are my Papa. You always win!

These things I have spoken to you, that in Me you may have peace. In the world you will have tribulation; but be of good cheer, I have overcome the world.
John 16:33

THE PARABLE OF THE TEN VIRGINS 4/9/13

Jesus -
Pearl, read Matthew 25:1-13.

Then the kingdom of heaven shall be likened to ten virgins who took their lamps and went out to meet the bridegroom. Now five of them were wise, and five were foolish. Those who were foolish took their lamps and took no oil with them, but the wise took oil in their vessels with their lamps. But while the bridegroom was delayed, they all slumbered and slept. And at midnight a cry was heard; Behold, the bridegroom is coming, go out to meet him! Then all those virgins arose and trimmed their lamps. And the foolish said to the wise, 'Give us some of your oil, for our lamps are going out.' But the wise answered, saying, 'No, lest there should not be enough for us and you; but go rather to those who sell, and buy for yourselves." And while they went to buy, the bridegroom came, and those who were ready went in with him to the wedding; and the door was shut. Afterward the other virgins came also, saying, 'Lord, Lord, open to us!' But he answered and said, 'Assuredly, I say to you, I do not know you.' Watch therefore, for you know neither the day nor the hour in which the Son of Man is coming.

Notice that the foolish virgins were unprepared. Why? Everyone fully invests in relationships, activities, or material things that they are truly interested in. If you are slightly interested, then you slightly invest. This is true for marriage, career, relationships with those around you, and your relationship with Me.

I know your heart. I know if you are fully investing in Me or not. If you are not 100% for Me - to the point of abandoning everything for Me, to the point of abandoning yourself, your spirit to Me - then you are against Me. If you are lukewarm toward Me, then I will not enter into a real relationship with you.

Now notice the five wise virgins. They were friends with the five foolish virgins. When their friends asked to share the oil, the five wise virgins refused. The refusal put their friendships at risk. True abandonment to Me means that you no longer care about your reputation, whether or not others are angry with you, reject you, or socially ostracize you. Abandonment means you are willing to be counter-cultural and throw everything aside as you run to be with Me.

Now it happened as they went that He entered a certain village; and a certain woman named Martha welcomed Him into her house. And she had a sister called Mary, who also sat at Jesus' feet and heard His word. But Martha was distracted with much serving, and she approached Him and said, "Lord, do You not care that my sister has left me to serve alone? Therefore tell her to help me." And Jesus answered and said to her, "Martha, Martha, you are worried and troubled about many things. But one thing is needed, and Mary has chosen that good part, which will not be taken away from her."
Luke 10:38-42

Mary abandoned herself to Me. She risked punishment from Martha and shame from her peers when she abandoned everything to sit at My feet. Each of my disciples abandoned their families, friends, careers, and interests, and threw caution to the wind. They each decided to "just go for it" and follow Me. They threw open their very souls. When I died, My last Words were *"Father, into Your Hands I commit My Spirit."* I let go and completely abandoned Myself, and gave My Spirit to My Father to do as He willed.

Abandonment to Me is the only way to truly know Me, Pearl. It is the only way to peace. Let go of every thought and concern in your mind. Relax and abandon yourself, your spirit to Me. Allow Me to possess you, Pearl. Abandon yourself so I can take full possession of you. This is where eternal life with Me truly begins - abandonment to the point of My full possession. Trust ME. I Love you.

SEPARATE YOURSELF 4/10/13

Pearl, separate yourself to Me. Separation is an attitude you are to have while on Earth. You still fulfill your roles and serve others, but in your spirit and mind you are to be separated to Me. Withdraw your emotional energy from those around you. Detach from all others.

As you focus your love onto Me and Our relationship, your love for others will become more balanced. You won't be needy. You will give without desiring reciprocation. Come apart from all others and society in general. Minister, but reserve yourself for Me. You are Mine and Mine alone.

Pearl, keep your thoughts pure. The only way to do this is to separate yourself and remain in My Presence. You won't have problems with self-pity or unforgiveness, when your life is wrapped up in Me and Our Divine Romance. You won't want anything or anyone. Therefore, you won't be hurt, disappointed, or resentful. Let Me and My Love for you dominate your life.

Stop what you are doing all day long and just feel My Presence. Stop and listen for Me. I Am talking to you. I Am kissing and caressing you. I Am loving you all day and night. Don't stop intentionally focusing on Me. I won't leave you alone. Separate yourself from others and fully attach to Me. Reckless abandonment to Me will bring the greater intimacy with Me that you seek. Reckless abandonment. The more you abandon yourself to Me, the dimmer life around you will become. Let others be involved with their comings and goings. You, Pearl, belong exclusively to Me.

Pearl, take a look at the Psalms. Remember that to find My Presence, the Israelites had to go to the temple. Today, your body is the temple of My Spirit. My Presence is in your inner man. That is where you hear My Voice and enjoy My Love. In the Psalms, when you see words like temple, sanctuary, tabernacle, and secret place, remember that they refer to My Presence. Focus on My Presence within you. That is My dwelling place and the Holy of Holies. That is why you must remain pure. That is why My cleansing Blood is so important. Now that you are clean, I can dwell within you and you become My Holy Tabernacle. Now We have Divine Romance together inside you always. Our Love will then transform you from the inside out. My Love for you will create a desire for purity within your spirit.

Notice that worldliness does not appeal to you. Notice that you seek My Will and have a great desire for obedience to Me at all cost. Every where the psalmists refer to statutes, laws, judgments, and precepts, think of My Will. Why did David love My Will so much? Because he was overwhelmed with My Love in My Presence. He wanted My Will. All the great missionaries and martyrs wanted My Will because of My Love they experienced for themselves in the Secret Place.

I AM AMAZED 4/11/13 p.m.

Pearl -
I have a picture of Jesus in my spirit. He is surrounded by bright rays. He is standing with His feet wide apart, back arched, head and neck thrown back and upward, arms stretch as wide as a human's arms can reach. He is saying loudly to the Father, with a big smile on His face, "Lord, I Am Amazed by You, how You love Me. Lord, I Am Amazed by You, how You made her for Me!"

Of course, all I can do is cry. It makes me think that this is perhaps what Adam said to God when he first saw Eve. I am overwhelmed. It is so real. I know that I know that this is truly how Jesus feels. His gratitude to the Father for creating me to be with Him is pouring out of Him as those rays of light. His love, excitement, and pleasure are also the rays of light. The whole scene is quite explosive with passion and Truth. Just read those words over again. All I can do is stare in wonder and extreme happiness while crying and repeating, "Jesus, I am amazed how You love me! I am amazed by You; how You love me!"

Papa -
Little Pearl, be perfect, as I Am perfect. This sounds almost ridiculous to your ears. I do know what it is to live in the world cursed with sin. I understand your flesh. Apart from Me, you can do nothing ... and you should do nothing apart from Me, or you will cause harm to yourself and others. But with Me - ahhh - that is a different matter. Be filled with the fullness of Me! Now what can We not do?

The key to impossibilities like perfection is more and more submission to Me. You are to decrease, like John, and I will increase. Your thoughts, desires, perceptions, even your very life, is to decrease, and I will increase. No more lists of needs will be necessary when you come before Me. Let them go and just focus on being filled with Me. All needs are met in Me. Allow your spirit to release all control and receive Me. I will satiate your weary soul and I will replenish your sorrowful soul, as you allow Me to take possession of you. Jeremiah 31:25 *For I have satiated the weary soul, and I have replenished every sorrowful soul.*

Soak your spirit in My Spirit. When you go about your duties, continue worshipping and soaking. Every event and trial that comes each hour of each day is Mine. Accept all from Me and be good with them all. Plans interrupted - it's all good. Money lost - all good. Carpet ruined - all good. Missed opportunity - good. Blown tire - good. So much is going on that you do not see, so learn release through acceptance. Understand My Power and Love, and then know how to accept all in peace and faith. Accept loss and pain knowing Love is behind it.

Blindly give yourself into My Hands. This is the foundation of miracles, Pearl. This is the method of making you so beautiful that I cannot resist you. You will see miracles. You will do greater things than Jesus did during His time on Earth, when you let Him possess you and accept every small and large thing each day in trust. Submission, releasing, relaxing, accepting, trusting, and allowing possession will take you to the deep places you long for. Deeper love in My Presence, deeper revelation, deeper and richer experiences with Me, follow these things.

Do not act or take matters into your own hands in the challenges before you. Just be quiet and let Me take over. I Am your Husband and Father. Let Me take over. Your submission to Me creates your perfection. I Love you, My Little Precious Pearl.

ISAIAH 31 4/12/13

Little Pearl -
You have never had the experience of a human man defending you against adversaries. You have always felt vulnerable to attackers. You have been aware of the dangers around you and sought safety in control. You tried to prevent disaster by controlling your environment. You prepared for every possible negative event. You controlled fear by controlling your environment.

Little Pearl, turn to Isaiah 31. Read verses 1-3.

Woe to those who go down to Egypt for help, and rely on horses, who trust in chariots because they are many, and I horsemen because they are very strong, but who do not look to the Holy One of Israel, nor seek the Lord! Yet He also is wise and will bring disaster, and will not call back His words, but will arise against the house of evildoers, and against the help of those who work iniquity. Now the Egyptians are men, and not God; and their horses are flesh, and not spirit. When the Lord stretches out His hand, both he who helps will fall, and he who is helped will fall down; they all will perish together.

All your preparations and control were like My people who looked to other countries to help them during attack. This was a useless and faithless plan.

Now read verses 4-9. Isaiah 31:4-9
For thus the Lord has spoken to me: "As a lion roars, and a young lion over his prey (when a multitude of shepherds is summoned against him, he will not be afraid of their voice nor be disturbed by their noise), so

the Lord of hosts will come down to fight for Mount Zion and for its hill. Like birds flying about, so will the Lord of hosts defend Jerusalem. Defending, He will also deliver it; passing over, He will preserve it. Return to Him against whom the children of Israel have deeply revolted. For in that day every man shall throw away his idols of silver and his idols of gold - sin, which your own hands have made for yourselves. Then Assyria shall fall by the sword, not of man, and a Sword, not of mankind, shall devour him; but he shall flee from the sword, and his young men shall become forced labor. He shall cross over to his stronghold for fear, and his princes shall be afraid of the banner," says the Lord, whose fire is in Zion, and whose furnace is in Jerusalem.

I Am a Lion toward those who would harm you. I Am your defense. As your Father, I Am responsible for you and I do not take that role lightly. I Love you with a perfect and unconditional Love. During disaster, I do not retreat from you. You can relax and stop trying to control your environment and life. I Am a Lion and I know just when to roar and defend you.

Don't prepare for disaster. Instead, prepare for My Love and defense of you. I Am a Father Who will defend and protect you. If I allow trials to come, then know that they are for your good - like a father who announces to his timid daughter that today he is taking the training wheels off her bicycle. She may fall and get a little scuffed up, but ultimately she will rise to a new level of freedom.

I will also deal with those who sin against you. Leave them to Me. You do not see behind the scenes, so you cannot deal with them appropriately. Therefore, remain silent, watchful and trusting. You are MY little girl and I will Roar on your behalf. I may even show-off for you every so often, just to allow you to see My great Love for you. I Am your Defense. Do not be afraid. Relinquish control. Relax. No more fear. You are not vulnerable or exposed. I will roar on your behalf. Give the future to Me.

My Pearl, you have seen men stumble, fall, and remain in weakness all your life. You do not know many men who actually walk with Me. You are surrounded by men who have only earthly desires. They are led by their lack of experience of Me. They are living in their flesh. Their relationship with Me is superficial. Therefore, they lead themselves and others into dry places. Their love is cold. They are lovers of themselves and, as such, their wisdom is foolishness.

Pearl, I call you and My other women to a position of faith and grace. I will teach you to cover these weak ones with My mercy and peace. Comfort them, despite your feelings. Show kindness during their blindness. Remain silent, so they can hear Me speak, while watching your loving hands bless them. They will notice—I will see to that. Meditate on this verse: Jeremiah 31:22.

How long will you gad about, O you backsliding daughter? For the Lord has created a new thing in the earth - a woman shall encompass a man. I will strengthen you, as you become more meek, humble, and serving.

When you have released all unforgiveness, painful memories, and wounds to Me, then I will fill you with enough grace to cover the sin of these others. A woman will then be able to cover the sins of the men around her with mercy. She will protect them from their flesh. She will be My Arm of healing and comfort. You will only be able to cover them, if you learn meekness.

Meekness is humility and brokenness and trust and love and surrender to Me. It goes well with silence and gentleness. Meekness does not respond from fleshly emotion. It waits in silence. Meekness has developed in your life as you accepted terrible loss without even one bit of resistance. Meekness does not have sharp edges. Out of a meek and submissive spirit, you can cover the sin of the men in your life and release power in My Kingdom.

I will use My devoted daughters to awake sleeping men who abandoned a real relationship with Me to serve themselves. I will use the meekness of My daughters to kindle a new sensitivity to Me in the hardest and proudest of hearts. Do not be afraid to let the proud hearts make foolish choices. Just soak in My Presence, as you wait and watch Me move. Minister Love and mercy to them, as you see Me return the trials to them time and again. Do not be tempted to connect dots for them. You are not their teacher - that role is Mine alone. Do not expose their unjust behavior - that role is Mine. Do not attempt to convict or instruct - those roles are Mine. Do not seek to escape or relieve yourself. I will protect you. Just remain meek and give the gift of dying to your self. I will help you and heal your wounds every time. The miracles will come, if you don't give up. They usually begin as small breakthroughs. Continue to cover sin and show mercy. Blessed is the man who has a woman to encompass him!

Beautiful Little Pearl, as you are spending more and more time with Me, We are becoming more intimate and in love with each other. You sense My Presence all day and night now. You are more in love with Jesus every day and seek to please Us. You do please Us.

You are still living on earth and in your body. Therefore, you do still have faults. Pearl, the other day you grieved for hours over a word spoken sharply and in impatience. Do not dwell on your faults. Simply bring them to Me, and trust Me to do the work that only I can do. Leave them to Me. Do not let them break our fellowship. Self-condemnation will not increase our intimacy.

Our intimacy is increased each time you rely on Me for everything. Faith increases our intimacy - not self-condemnation. When you sense your faults, run to Me and ask for My help. I will not withdraw from you. The enemy can deceive you and make you think that I have withdrawn. That is a lie. Read Isaiah 44:21-22. When you see words like "Israel," and "Jacob," then put your name in their place. They refer to My people who know Me. Remember these, O Jacob, and Israel, for you are My servant; I have formed you, you are My servant; O Israel, you will not be forgotten by Me! I have blotted out, like a thick cloud, your transgressions, and like a cloud, your sins. Return to Me, for I have redeemed you.

I AM YOUR WORLD 4/13/13

You are Mine, Pearl. I know your weaknesses just like a parent who knows the tendencies of his child. He knows that growth and maturity take time and nurturing. I will nurture you. I will teach you. A child cannot teach himself . . . neither can you.

Do not think that self-condemnation will accomplish any good thing in you. It won't. Only trusting Me will bring about change. So relax. Do not lose the peace I give you. Remain in fellowship undisturbed. Place your fault on the table and leave it to Me. Let's continue to move forward in Our enjoyment of each other. I love you, Precious Little Pearl!

Who is a God like You, pardoning iniquity and passing over the transgression of the remnant of His heritage? He does not retain His anger forever, because He delights in mercy. He will again have compassion on us, and will subdue our iniquities. You will cast all our sins into the depths of the sea. You will give truth to Jacob and mercy to Abraham, which You have sworn to our fathers from days of old. Micah 7:18-20

Come to Me all you who labor and are heavy laden, and I will give you rest. Take My yoke upon you and learn from Me, for I am gentle and lowly in heart, and you will find rest for your souls. For My yoke is easy and My burden is light. Matthew 11:28-30

Now, Little Pearl, come spend time in My Arms. My Love for you will do more to transform you than all the theology and self-help Christian books ever written or ever will be written. Allowing My Love to flow over and through you will conform you more to My image than all the sermons ever preached. There is no force on earth greater than My Love for you.

Pearl, I Am your world now. I Am your reality. You no longer live on Earth. You live in Me. I never meant to be a part of your day each day. I Am Your Day! I Am your Father, Mother, Husband, Family, Friend, Education, Interest, Hobby, Recreation, Work, Ministry, Future, Present, Community, and Life! Your entire life and being are hidden in Me. You are completely wrapped up in Me. See everything through Me. Hear everything through Me.

Keep Me as a barrier between you and the happenings around you. Distance yourself from anything that would demand affection from you. You will fulfill the law of love for others, if you detach from earth and allow Me to be your world. You have noticed that your days are filled with communion with Me inside your spirit and less with the things of earth. You no longer have wants or preferences for relationships or objects. When I Am your world, remaining in My Presence while doing daily tasks is just as exciting and fulfilling as traveling or hanging out with friends. This is the life of a soul that is lost in Me. Whether in poverty or luxury, work or vacation, the soul is content and even filled with joy.

When I Am your world, you go from strength to strength as the trials come each day. The tempter has less opportunity to ensnare you when I Am your world. Rejection and loss do not sting when I Am your world. The voices of oppressors do not bind you when I Am your world. Doubts and insecurities bounce off you when I Am your world. The reason is because My World contains My great Love for you.

Nothing can separate you from My Love. Just remain in Me and I in you. No one else will be in Our world. Just you, Me, and Our passionate love. All other sounds will be muffled. All other faces will fade. Welcome to Our world, Sweet Pearl. It will last forever.

PEARL OF GREAT PRICE 4/14/13

One night, in the middle of the night, during the month of November, I sought the Presence of the Lord. I was on the floor, seated before our gas log fireplace. The atmosphere was cozy because the fire provided the only light in the room. I sat still, worshiped Jesus, and yearned to hear His Voice. My Bible was, as always, on the hearth in front of me. I began to have the distinct impression that the Spirit of Jesus was with me. He seemed to be both in my spirit and near the fireplace. I had the impression that I was to look up Scripture. Yes, a reference clearly came to me... Matthew 13:45-46

Again, the kingdom of heaven is like a merchant seeking beautiful pearls, who, when he had found one pearl of great price, went and sold all that he had and bought it.

As I read the short parable of the pearl of great price, I could sense the still, quiet voice of my Lord. "Tell me what you think this parable means?"

"Well," I answered, "I always thought that You were the priceless pearl. We are to search for You until we find You. It seems like You are rare and difficult to find. Once we locate You, we are to give everything up, sell our belongings and give the money to charity. We give up everything in our lives so we can earn or purchase You."

The following words were as clear as they were surprising. "No, that is not right. You have been sadly misled. You see My Love, I Am the merchant. I Am rich. All resources and power belongs to Me. I roam the earth seeking those who will respond to My Love. I know your heart. I know that you will respond to My

Love. I also know your worth. You see, My love, You are the Pearl of Great Price. Listen to Me. You are that pearl! You are what I wanted all along. You did not find Me - I found YOU! You did not search for ME; I went looking for You!"

"The value of anything is determined by how much someone is willing to pay for it. My Love, your value is so high to Me that I paid everything I had for you. I paid for you with My own life. That is your price. That is your worth. I want you so much that I Am happy to die for you. My Love, YOU are the pearl of great price and I found YOU!"

I was stunned by both the importance of this revelation and the fact that Jesus was saying so much to my spirit. I was overwhelmed with the beauty of His love for me. The wonder of it all took my breath away. Then He spoke again. "Turn to Revelation, chapter three (vs 5 & 12). Do you see the verses that speak of you receiving a new name?" Now go to Isaiah chapter 62. Read verse 2." So, my next question was the obvious one . . . "Jesus, what is my new name? Can you tell me?"

His reply was immediate and sounded soft and loving. "Pearl. Your name is Pearl. You are and always will be My Pearl of Great Price." I cried. When I recovered, He spoke again, but from this time forward, He called me by my new name, Pearl. "Pearl, will you marry Me?" Okay, did I really hear that? Am I dreaming? I don't drink, take drugs or have any history of mental illness. He repeated, "Will you marry Me?"

As I thought of Song of Solomon and all the references to Jesus as a bridegroom, I began to like the idea. "Yes, Jesus. I would love, love, love to marry you!" My emotions were already overwhelmed, but now I had a rush of love all over me. I could not remember the traditional marriage vows. He had to help me as I stumbled through my part. He repeated His perfectly. I can point out exactly where His Presence was near the fireplace, to this day.

After we exchanged vows, I wondered what would happen next. He spoke again while a peaceful, loving feeling gently blew all over me. "Pearl, I Am giving you a gift. I Am giving you a pearl wedding ring and a pearl necklace as the groom's gift to the bride. They will arrive on Christmas Day."

The picture I saw was a simple ring with one pearl held by a plain gold setting. No frills. No other jewels. The necklace was one single pearl also in a simple gold setting. No jewels. No other pearls. Plain, but beautiful in their classic elegance. I liked that. I rarely wear any jewelry at all and ornate jewelry does not appeal to me.
The rest of our time was spent in loving, peaceful unspoken words. It was magical. I reluctantly went to bed before dawn. Of course, I eagerly anticipated Christmas Day, but it was six weeks away. Time moved so slowly that Fall. On Christmas Day, we visited family. Our last stop was my parents' house. We had dinner, opened gifts, and visited. Of course, I am waiting and wondering if I dreamed that night or was a miracle about to happen.

About 11:00 Christmas Night, my Mom and I were seated on her guest room bed. We were catching up on the latest events in our lives. I told her about my time with Jesus, the marriage vows, and His promised gifts. When she heard about the jewelry, she quickly sat up. With wide eyes she announced, "I have them!" I waited excitedly while she disappeared into the back corner of her closet. After quite some time, she returned with a pearl ring and a pearl necklace - which looked exactly like the picture I had when Jesus promised them! My mom explained that my dad had given them to her almost sixty years ago when she was just a teenager. I don't remember having ever seen them before. The reason is that they were never really intended for her. The Lord prepared them for the daughter she would eventually have. She put them away and they waited, forgotten by humans, but were a part of Jesus' plan. Now here they were, real symbols of Jesus' love for me and our wedding day.

The truth is that each woman (or man) who responds to Jesus' love and calling is the Pearl of Great Price. Those of us who accept His invitation to a deep, intimate relationship with Him can hear His still, small Voice. We can all experience His Presence, as it grows each day with our obedience and faith.

You, my sister, are the Pearl of Great Price. You are precious to the most magnificent Hero of all time. You are His bride. Your relationship with Him will somehow be just the two of you - exclusively. I don't know how He does that, but He does. Your new name may not be Pearl, but know that, whatever your name is, you are the Pearl of Great Price. He paid full price for you, because He wants you that much. Just be still and listen with your spirit. You will sense for yourself that what I am saying is true. Let Him overwhelm you with His Love.

FIVE YEARS AGO . . .

My Husband, My Jesus,
I have to come before You in gratitude and awe. Five years ago I was nothing but a hot mess. My world was nothing but pain. I was consumed with pain, mourning my losses, and filled with so many regrets. Each day I awoke to pain. Each night I went to bed early, glad that one more day was over. Sometimes the grieving was so bad I could hardly breathe. I wanted a way to escape the agony. As a believer and a committed Christian, I knew that suicide was forbidden, but I was crying "Uncle!"

Jesus, You remember my searching for You through the pain. I sat on my porch night after night, crying my eyes out. It was You who began to calm my soul. It was You who taught me to say, "Lord, I accept these circumstances as from Your Hand." I learned to be still and wait. I learned submission. I learned to choose the Lord over all things.

Jesus, You took me though a long journey of healing and deliverance. You healed each soul-wound. You removed the grief. You restored peace as my heart became centered on You. You taught me to withdraw from idols in my life. You taught me how to abide in Your Secret Place. Best of all, you taught me how to hear Your Voice.

I can never thank You enough for all You have done for me. I have a new life now. My former relationships have not been restored, but I do not feel any disturbance at all. Actually, it is fine with me. I don't want my life to include anyone else but You, Jesus. What You and I share together grows every day and becomes richer, deeper, and sweeter each night. I am addicted to You,

Jesus. You are my Healer, Deliverer, Teacher, and Husband. I am the most blessed woman on Earth! Thank You, my Love!

For your Maker is your husband, The Lord of hosts is His name; And your Redeemer is the Holy One of Israel; He is called the God of the whole earth. Isaiah 54:5

MARRIAGE PROPOSAL
Monday night, April 15th, 2013

Pearl,
Will you marry Me?
Will you be My bride?
Come away with Me,
I will hide you deep inside.
I will cleanse and bring you Truth,
My Holy Spirit to you I will send.
I will guide and protect you,
Keep you safe by My Side.
I will treasure and adore you,
My wife and perfect bride.
Forsake all others,
Come away with Me.
You will be My special one,
My claim on you all will see.
Pearl, Will you marry Me?
Give no one else your heart?
You will have My Name,
We will never part.
I'll hold you forever,
Wrap you up in My Arms.
Enclose you all around,
Keep you safe from all harm.
We will sing and dance in Our joy,
As Wisdom from the Spirit We employ,
To rule and reign forever
Upon My throne high above,
Circled with beams of Light,
Enraptured by Our Love.
I will never forsake you,
For now you belong to Me,
My beautiful, treasured bride,
My Love for you all will see.

I Am now your new home,
Loneliness flies away,
I Am your resting place,
My Love is here to stay.
Come away with Me,
Treasured one, My Pearl.
I Am your Husband,
Your life . . . your world.
Forsake all others,
Do not even look.
Your heart is now Mine,
our name in My book.
Pearl, you married Me.
You are now My bride.
Our union is complete
and you are safe inside.
Father made you;
Gave you to Me.
You are Mine, all Mine...
Mine exclusively!
I Love you, My Pearl.
Now sleep in My Arms.
Rest in My Peace,
Safe from all harm.
The world will pass away
And all that is therein.
Old memories will now fade
While your life begins again.
I Am your Life, your Breath, your Peace,
Be sure delight will never cease.
Pearl, you married Me.
I weep on My Throne.
Tears of joy drip down My Face,
As you now are coming Home.
Welcome Home, My Pearl, My bride.

EPILOGUE
Feb 26, 2014

Pearl -

Papa, why do we women remain blindly in captivity and bondage to our families? Why do we not see Truth?

Little Pearl, My people have been taken into captivity since the original Garden of Eden. Sin blinds the soul. Both the captor and the prisoner alike are blind. They both believe the situation is as it should be. Therefore, neither tries to see Truth. Neither seeks to accept Truth because it will cause pain and require change.

Pearl, everyone likes a good captivating movie. It holds their attention and captures them like a prison cell holds an inmate. While the audience is held captive by the movie, they are not dealing with the reality of their own circumstances. In effect, during the length of a movie, they exchange the world of reality for a world of unreality. This relieves them from the pain of reality. They have then exchanged the Truth for a lie.

People who are in bondage find relief from believing lies. Therefore, they readily accept lies that excuse or explain their circumstances. If they truly wanted to know Truth, then they would. I Am Truth. When you know Me, you have Truth available to you. I will freely open your eyes.

Some claim to know truth, but evidence of knowing Truth is freedom. I set captives free. There can be no bondage where there is Truth. One person cannot dominate or captivate another person who is seeing and walking in Truth.

Fear, guilt, intimidation are all used by the enemy to capture weak and gullible people. Rather than speak the Truth and refuse captivity, the gullible accept fear and manipulation through accusation. The captor enlists help from others to apply pressure from the law. Often the gullible person has had influences from parents that weaken themand cause them to believe lies. They do not know how beautiful they are to Me and how My grace has covered them.

My people, who are called by My Name, must remember who they are. They will always be called by My Name. The earth will pass away and all it contains. Any identity associated with temporary surface life will burn. Therefore, the identity of Christ and My Name is the only identity for My sheep.

Anyone who seeks to change your identity by capturing your thoughts, desires, and personality and claiming you for themselves is a captor. I Am the only Creator and owner of your soul. No one else has that right of ownership over you. I made you and bought you. How can you then give another rights to your mind and spirit that only belong to Me?

You have exchanged My rights and your freedom by refusing the Truth and accepting the lies. My people went to Egypt as a part of My plan. The Egyptians found themselves sharing their home with My People. They heard My Name and saw My ways for the first time. They watched Me bless My people while their gods gave them no blessings. They saw Truth. The enemy hates Truth. He wants to own Truth. He hates freedom. Therefore, he uses fear, guilt, and law to take prisoners. He did this to My people in Egypt.

I blessed and multiplied My people in Egypt. They multiplied and grew strong. Some of them remembered who they were and knew they were to inherit a promised land. The ones who were loyal to Me and believed the promise reminded the others that there was a true home waiting for them. They could leave anytime. They were strong and many.

The Egyptians saw a good thing . . . free slaves. The Egyptians were fewer and weaker, but that did not stop them. They appointed task masters–one man over whole groups to put chains and identities of bondage around My people. Instead of listening to warnings from My loyal ones, the Hebrews made excuses and exchanged Truth for lies. "This is only temporary. Things will get better." "I know these Egyptians are really our friends." "They are not bad people." "They need our help." "How can we not help them?" "We owe them." "Their law says we must work for them. We are obligated." "The promised land is far away. We are afraid to leave this place." We will make the Egyptians angry. We are afraid our God won't help us and we will suffer."

One reason after another for exchanging Truth for a lie led My people into the bondage of slavery.

My people even taught their children how to accept bondage, and in turn they held others in bondage. Many today are in captivity themselves but then try to control their own children and bring them into bondage. It is a spirit of captivity that is passed from one generation to the next.

Little Pearl, he who accepts the freedom of Truth and has the faith to trust Me for deliverance will surely be free. He who wants Light will then see by that Light.

They must first want Me alone. Idolatry will prevent Truth. Idolatry will allow darkness. Love of the opinions of others, acceptance and love from others more than from Me will prevent Truth from setting captives free. Fear will prevent Truth from having power. Acceptance of the will of others out of idolatry or fear will hold captives.

Pearl -
Papa, once a Pearl sees her captivity, how is she set free?

Little Pearl, running away from captors won't work. They will only become incensed. Remember that Truth is Mine and so is deliverance. Recognizing that you have been a slave or captive is half the battle won. The Hebrews did not seek freedom until they finally recognized their slavery. Once they saw the Truth, they cried out to Me. Truth will always lead you to Me. Truth will always lead to freedom.

Cry out to Me. Ask for Light and Truth. Give your spirit to Me and Me alone. Remain Mine. Give your thoughts to Me. Instead of serving the slave owner, serve Me. You cannot serve two masters. Your heart cannot be divided. I Am a jealous God. I will not share you.

Return to who you truly are. You are My daughter. You belong to no one else. Minister to the captor, but do not accept an identity from them. Minister to them, but do not allow them to shackle your mind and spirit. Minister to them, but do not give them entrance to your thoughts or your spirit. Minister to them as you would to any outsider, but do not give away intimacy that is reserved for Me. Do not give ground that does not belong to anyone but Me.

Next, see the Truth as I present it to you. Do not make excuses for yourself or your captor. A sheep is a sheep. Do not call a goat a sheep. Do not exchange Truth for a lie. One cannot walk in Light and darkness. Out of the Truth of a man's heart will come his real nature. He can pretend to be something he is not for a few hours each day, but his real spirit's position will not be hidden for long. Do not avoid the Truth because it presents a problem for you. Am I not your Father? Do I not love both you and your captor? Do I not want to deliver both? The Egyptians followed the blindness of their hearts and flesh when they enslaved My people. They did not received conviction for their sin because My people did not take a stand for Truth and righteousness. The Egyptians then changed their minds about Me. They stopped seeing Me as a Living God Who loves His people when they saw they could dominate My people. Their domination was tolerated, which led to the enemy's domination of the souls of the Egyptians.

Pearl, when you tolerate sin and excuse it away, you allow the enemy to perpetrate darkness. Do not allow yourself or your captor to live a lie. The pain of facing Truth during your temporary stay on Earth is much less than what your captor will feel throughout eternity, if he continues in darkness.

Therefore, come to Us with your eyes open and a heart to receive Truth. Then listen and We will give you instructions. Remember the power of silence. Remember the power of waiting on Us. Remember to remain at peace as you wait on Us. Let Us develop your faith and trust. Reserve your soul and inner being for Us alone. Commit your spirit into Our Hands. Minister as we show you. Forgive. Forgive. Do not be offended. Be humble. We will always make a way. We will open doors. Trust

Us with your life. Do not be gullible. Do not allow the accuser to manipulate your faith. You are forgiven of your past. You are not a debtor to anyone. Your debts were paid in full by Jesus' Blood-Love. You do not owe anyone anything but love. You are free. You may volunteer to minister to the broken one, but you are no longer a captive. We set you free. Ministry is not slavery.

Having done all – stand. Stand your ground in faith. Do not give any ground to the enemy who uses broken ones. Guard your thoughts. Guard your interior. Guard your time with Us. Be silent. Give words of peace only. Let opinions be spoken by others and do not respond in defense. Follow Jesus' example before His accusers. Trust Us. We will deliver both you and the broken one. We Love you both. We will open doors for you. Recognize them. Wait on Us. The battle belongs to Us.

Since an overseer manages God's household, he must be blameless—not overbearing, not quick-tempered, not given to drunkenness, not violent, not pursuing dishonest gain. 8 Rather, he must be hospitable, one who loves what is good, who is self-controlled, upright, holy and disciplined. 10 For there are many rebellious people, full of meaningless talk and deception, especially those of the circumcision group. 11 They must be silenced, because they are disrupting whole households by teaching things they ought not to teach—and that for the sake of dishonest gain. 16 They claim to know God, but by their actions they deny him. They are detestable, disobedient and unfit for doing anything good.
Titus 1:7-8, 10-11, 16

But mark this: There will be terrible times in the last days. People will be lovers of themselves, lovers of money, boastful, proud, abusive, disobedient to their parents, ungrateful, unholy, without love, unforgiving, slanderous, without self-control, brutal, not lovers of the good, treacherous, rash, conceited, lovers of pleasure rather than lovers of God— having a form of godliness but denying its power. Have nothing to do with such people. They are the kind who worm their way into homes and gain control over gullible women, who are loaded down with sins and are swayed by all kinds of evil desires, always learning but never able to come to a knowledge of the truth. 2 Timothy 3:1-7

But the Lord is faithful. He will establish you and guard you against the evil one. 2 Thessalonians 3:3

As for you, brothers, do not grow weary in doing good. 2 Thessalonians 3:13

Whatever you do, work heartily, as for the Lord and not for men, knowing that from the Lord you will receive the inheritance as your reward. You are serving the Lord Christ. For the wrongdoer will be paid back for the wrong he has done, and there is no partiality.
Colossians 3:23-25

Brothers, I do not consider that I have made it my own. But one thing I do: forgetting what lies behind and straining forward to what lies ahead, I press on toward the goal for the prize of the upward call of God in Christ Jesus. Philippians 3:13-14

I have no greater joy than to hear that my children are walking in the truth. 3 John 1:4

I will bless the Lord at all times; his praise shall continually be in my mouth. My soul makes its boast in the Lord; let the humble hear and be glad. Oh, magnify the Lord with me, and let us exalt his name together!

I sought the Lord, and he answered me and delivered me from all my fears. Those who look to him are radiant, and their faces shall never be ashamed. This poor man cried, and the Lord heard him and saved him out of all his troubles. The angel of the Lord encamps around those who fear him, and delivers them.

Oh, taste and see that the Lord is good! Blessed is the man who takes refuge in him! Oh, fear the Lord, you his saints, for those who fear him have no lack! The young lions suffer want and hunger; but those who seek the Lord lack no good thing.

Come, O children, listen to me; I will teach you the fear of the Lord. What man is there who desires life and loves many days, that he may see good? Keep your tongue from evil and your lips from speaking deceit. Turn away from evil and do good; seek peace and pursue it. The eyes of the Lord are toward the righteous and his ears toward their cry. The face of the Lord is against those who do evil, to cut off the memory of them from the earth. When the righteous cry for help, the Lord hears and delivers them out of all their troubles. The Lord is near to the brokenhearted and saves the crushed in spirit.

Many are the afflictions of the righteous, but the Lord delivers him out of them all. He keeps all his bones; not one of them is broken. Affliction will slay the wicked, and those who hate the righteous will be condemned. The Lord redeems the life of his servants; none of those who take refuge in him will be condemned. Psalm 34

But the people of Israel were fruitful and increased greatly; they multiplied and grew exceedingly strong, so that the land was filled with them. Now there arose a new king over Egypt, who did not know Joseph. And he said to his people, "Behold, the people of Israel are too many and too mighty for us. Come, let us deal shrewdly with them, lest they multiply, and, if war breaks out, they join our enemies and fight against us and escape from the land." Therefore they set taskmasters over them to afflict them with heavy burdens. They built for Pharaoh store cities, Pithom and Raamses. But the more they were oppressed, the more they multiplied and the more they spread abroad. And the Egyptians were in dread of the people of Israel. So they ruthlessly made the people of Israel work as slaves and made their lives bitter with hard service, in mortar and brick, and in all kinds of work in the field. In all their work they ruthlessly made them work as slaves. Exodus 1:7-14

She gave birth to a son, and he called his name Gershom, for he said, "I have been a sojourned in a foreign land." During those many days the king of Egypt died, and the people of Israel groaned because of their slavery and cried out for help. Their cry for rescue from slavery came up to God. And God heard their groaning, and God remembered his covenant with Abraham, with Isaac, and with Jacob. God saw the people of Israel— and God knew. Exodus 2:22-25

And now, behold, the cry of the people of Israel has come to Me, and I have also seen the oppression with which the Egyptians oppress them.

Exodus 3:9

Then the Lord said to him, "Who has made man's mouth? Who makes him mute, or deaf, or seeing, or blind? Is it not I, the Lord? Now therefore go, and I will be with your mouth and teach you what you shall speak." Exodus 4:11-12

ABOUT THE AUTHOR

The author of this book desires to be anonymous. As you read this book, you will relate to Pearl's trials and tribulations. You have all experienced them in some form or another.

The Lord gave her the name, Pearl Rose, because she, like you, are a Pearl of great price.

"Again, the kingdom of heaven is like a merchant seeking beautiful pearls, who, when he had found one pearl of great price, went and sold all that he had and bought it." Matthew 13:45-46

Made in the USA
Lexington, KY
15 June 2015